The Waddesdon Bequest

The Legacy of Baron Ferdinand Rothschild to the British Museum

Hugh Tait

Published for the Trustees of the British Museum
by British Museum Publications Ltd

Front cover: Late Renaissance Taste: a selection of precious objects from the Waddesdon Bequest, including a Limoges painted enamel casket by Susanne Court, a knife and fork with gold enamelled handles recording a wedding between two noble families in the Netherlands, a Spanish gold 'mermaid' pendant set with emeralds and diamonds, an Italian sardonyx cameo set in a gold pendant jewel framed with rubies, a silver-gilt triangular salt-cellar in the sophisticated Mannerist style of Wenzel Jamnitzer, a variegated agate tazza with gem-set gold enamelled mounts and an enamelled gold medal struck in commemoration of the Order of the Garter being conferred on the Prince of Orange by King Charles I of England in 1627.

Back cover: The north front of Waddesdon Manor, the Buckinghamshire home of Baron Ferdinand Rothschild, MP. Building began after the death of his father, Baron Anselm, in 1874, and a grand house-warming took place in July, 1883. Queen Victoria herself spent the day there in May, 1890. In the smoking room of the bachelor's wing (to the extreme left of the photograph), the Baron created his great cabinet of Renaissance and earlier works of art; it was the contents of this room that he bequeathed to the British Museum to be known as the Waddesdon Bequest.

Fifty-nine years later his great-nephew, Mr James de Rothschild, was to leave to the nation not only Waddesdon Manor and its park but also the combined collections of his inheritance from Baron Edmond (of Paris) and from Baron Ferdinand's sister, Miss Alice. The result is a house particularly rich in French eighteenth-century art but with many other facets too. Now part of the National Trust, Waddesdon Manor may be visited from the last Wednesday in March to the last Sunday in October each year (Wednesdays–Sundays, 2pm–6pm; closed on Mondays and Tuesdays, except Bank Holidays).

© 1981 The Trustees of the British Museum

Published by British Museum Publications Ltd.
46 Bloomsbury Street, London WC1B 3QQ

British Library Cataloguing in Publication Data
Tait, Hugh
    The Waddesdon Bequest.
    1. Art objects – London (England)
    – Exhibitions
    I. Title   II. British Museum
    709.02′4   NK480.L67
    ISBN 0-7141-1357-3

Designed by James Shurmer

Set in Monophoto Baskerville and printed in Great Britain by Jolly & Barber Ltd, Rugby

Contents

List of Illustrations

The numbers in brackets refer to *The Catalogue of the Waddesdon Bequest* by C.H. Read (London, 1902).

Preface

The aim has been to present a bird's eye view of the Waddesdon Bequest. No selection can perfectly mirror the multifarious riches of the Collection, but this choice reflects the most significant aspects while at the same time illustrating the themes that unite these works of art and the historical and technical backgrounds that made their creation possible. Every object will appear in the forthcoming volumes of the *Catalogue of the Waddesdon Bequest*, with detailed descriptions, complete bibliographical references and full discussion of the supporting evidence for the dating and attributions of origin, but the results of many new discoveries and reappraisals have been incorporated in this survey. I should like to take this opportunity of acknowledging my debt to the many learned authors whose specialist publications have clearly provided so much valuable information.

In addition, I wish to record my gratitude to the late Mr Tom Wragg, the Librarian and Keeper of the Devonshire Collections, without whose generous co-operation the comparative studies of the drawings in Chatsworth and London would not have been possible, and to Mr John Gere, Keeper of Prints and Drawings at the British Museum, for his expert opinion of these drawings, to His Honour Judge Stucley for his help based on his current study of the life of Sir Bevil Grenville, Richard Marks for his contribution to establishing the likely origin of the St Catherine figure, and Judith Swaddling for her reconsideration of the four Hellenistic bronzes. I should also like to express my deep appreciation of the work of those colleagues in the Geological Museum, especially Mr E. A. Jobbins, and in the Research Laboratory of the British Museum, who have helped to identify gem-stones and materials, and of the staff of the Photographic Service, who took many new photographs for this publication. My special thanks go to the staff of British Museum Publications Ltd, in particular to Celia Clear and Deborah Wakeling, and to the staff of my own Department, whose patient and often unglamorous assistance throughout has made this publication possible. Above all, I am especially indebted to Mrs James de Rothschild, the oldest living member of the Rothschild family and the closest in spirit to the subject of this survey, for her deep understanding and constant support.

1. Introduction

Baron Ferdinand Rothschild's ambition to possess a great room filled with precious objects of art of the highest quality, in the tradition of the Renaissance courts of Europe, had been so successful that, although he died at the early age of fifty-nine in 1898, he had not only more than trebled the size of the collection he had inherited from his father, but he was able to bequeath to the British Museum a collection that in most respects could have come straight from the *Schatzkammer* (or treasure-house) of a German prince of the Renaissance. For this reason, Baron Ferdinand's Bequest, seen separately as a single entity, serves to evoke and illustrate a facet of Renaissance court life, highlighting aspects of extravagant patronage, of ostentatious wealth, of curiosity in bizarre and exotic natural phenomena and, above all, of admiration for virtuosity in craftsmanship.

Baron Ferdinand (1839–98) was the grandson of the founder of the Austrian branch of the great Frankfurt banking house of Rothschild, and from his father, Baron Anselm of Vienna, he was to inherit in 1874 the nucleus of this magnificent collection. From his mother, who was English, he seems to have inherited a love of this country for, although born in Paris and brought up in Frankfurt and Vienna, he decided, at the age of twenty-one, to settle in England and make his life here. Five years later, he married his English cousin, Evelina, who tragically died in childbirth soon afterwards; he never married again. In public life, he was active as a Justice of the Peace and as a member of the Buckinghamshire County Council; he became High Sheriff of the County and for fourteen years was the Member of Parliament for the Aylesbury division of the County; he also served as a Trustee of the British Museum (see frontispiece).

Undoubtedly, the greatest single benefaction to the Museum in the field of Renaissance *objets d'art* occurred when Baron Ferdinand Rothschild died in 1898. His great collection, bequeathed on condition that it should be displayed in a room separate and apart from the other contents of the Museum, comprised all the works of art in the new smoking room in the so-called Bachelors' Wing at Waddesdon Manor, the imposing country house that the Baron had built in Buckinghamshire between 1874 and 1883, and, in accordance with his wishes, the collection is known as 'The Waddesdon Bequest'.

This Bequest, with its rich and varied selection totalling almost 300 items, serves to illustrate how Renaissance court patronage demanded from its craftsmen far more than mere competence; whatever the medium, craftsmanship had to excel itself, adding technical bravura to fantasy in design. It is this quality that dominates and unites the extraordinarily disparate elements of the Bequest and, when designing the display (Fig. 1) in the new Waddesdon Room (opened in 1973), my aim was to create an element of surprise and wonder as befits objects that were, for the most part, originally made for a *Kunst-und-Wunder-Kammer*, a room of precious curiosities and works of art, such as almost every Renaissance court in Europe possessed before the end of the sixteenth century.

Fig. 1 The new Waddesdon Room at the British Museum: a corner showing part of the plate displayed in the outer room and a section of the Renaissance jewellery and microscopic wood and honestone carvings arranged in the more intimate setting of the inner room.

Fig. 2 Plan of the Waddesdon Room at the British Museum numbered to accompany the text describing the arrangement of the collection (see opposite). Top arrow on plan indicates view shown in Fig. 1.

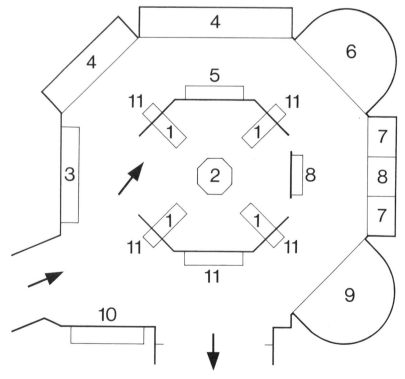

On entering the new Waddesdon Room, the eye is led, by means of special lighting, colour and case design, to dwell on the intricate and often minute details of exquisite workmanship. By placing the objects very close to the eye in these conditions, the brilliance of the execution and the mastery of the material can be appreciated and Fig.2(1) enjoyed. The many small-scale objects, like the Renaissance jewels and the miniature carvings in boxwood and honestone, are arranged within an inner octagonal room that not only has a more intimate atmosphere but also provides all-round vision for most of them. At the centre of this inner room, the greatest jewel of the Bequest, the gold Fig.2(2) enamelled and gem-studded Reliquary of the Holy Thorn made for Jean, duc de Berry, about 1405, is displayed on its own and is skilfully lit from above and below so that even the now faint, but elaborately pounced, decoration on the golden doors of St Michael and St Christopher at the back can be discerned.

In the outer room are grouped the larger objects in the Bequest. Immediately to the Fig.2(3) left of the entrance, a case contains the four highly decorated guns, the longest of which measures 5 ft 8 in (1.73 m). Beyond, on two walls of the outer octagon, is amassed the finest array of German and Netherlandish Renaissance silver plate to be seen in Fig.2(4) England. It includes, in the centre of the first section, those remarkable curiosities, like nautilus shells, ostrich eggs and unusual minerals, which the goldsmiths have imaginatively mounted in silver and gold, thereby transforming them into objects of fantasy and delight. Continuing past the silver plate, opposite which are displayed three Fig.2(5) masterpieces of medieval metalwork, there is a large open alcove containing Italian Fig.2(6) maiolica of the mid-sixteenth century and two contemporary Italian bronze door-knockers of elegant Mannerist design. The maiolica, a tin-glazed pottery with richly coloured painted decoration, includes several large-scale items of high quality that testify to the skill of the potters of Urbino at that time.

Along the next side of the outer octagon are gathered most of the French Renais-Fig.2(7) sance painted enamels in the Bequest. In the main, they depict, in strong vibrant colours, scenes of classical mythology copied from contemporary engravings by Italian and French artists, though the backs tend to be finely painted in grisaille (a white-on-black technique) with intricate Mannerist ornamental designs filled with strange grotesques. Similar ornament can be seen on some of the Italian gold-damascened Fig.2(8) ironwork, which is displayed in the central section of this side of the Room; for example, on the famous shield signed by Giorgio Ghisi, of Mantua, and dated 1554, which is a *tour de force* in this technique.

Fig.2(9) In a second open alcove are displayed the two large wooden sculptures of St George and St Catherine, and an iron coffer, all in the Late Gothic style. To the right of the Fig.2(10) exit a specially designed show-case is lit partly from behind so that the engraved rock-crystals and the important glass vessels may be seen to full advantage; at either side of this case, the special lighting helps to illuminate the subtle modelling of four Hellenistic bronze heads, the amber tankard and some of the smaller painted enamels. Finally, the Fig.2(11) exterior walls of the inner octagon have been used for the display of the finest wood-carvings, including the very impressive pair of portrait busts of Margaret of Austria and Philibert of Savoy and four other small-scale wood-carvings of exceptional merit, each of which is shown separately in an individual case. Of the four, perhaps the most sculptural is the seated figure of Omphale, in which the sculptor, Arthus Quellinus the elder, reveals above all the dominant influence of Rubens, whose busy workshop in the Netherlands served in so grand a manner not only his powerful patron, the Archduke

11

Albert, brother of the Emperor Rudolph II, but many other courts of Europe, even London where the ceiling of the Banqueting Hall in Whitehall was painted with an elaborate and recondite scheme extolling the virtues of a King by Divine Right, James I of England and VI of Scotland.

In England, the belated but not unimpressive attempts of Charles I to vie with the magnificence of the Hapsburgs and the Wittelsbachs, for example, came to a sudden and disastrous end, for after the Civil War the victorious Cromwell sold what remained of the English *Schatzkammer*. Virtually nothing escaped; only the long lists in the old Royal inventories with their dry, brief descriptions testify to the lost splendours of the treasuries of the courts of the Tudors and the Stuarts. A jewel, like the exquisite diamond-studded locket that James I gave to a Somerset gentleman, Thomas Lyte, in 1610, which now hangs in the Waddesdon Bequest, is but a tiny token of the lavish gestures that formed the ostentatious pattern of life at the courts of Renaissance Europe. Indeed, as a form of propaganda, these treasuries of the ruling dynasties served to convey both a sense of their power and stability and their civilised cultivation of the arts and of learning. The Room of the Waddesdon Bequest re-creates this princely taste, with its uneasy combination of artistic patronage and blatant emphasis on wealth.

2. Objects of Pre-Renaissance Date

In addition to all the Renaissance *objets d'art* in the Waddesdon Bequest, there are a few exceptionally important medieval objects of the kind which can still be seen, for example, in the *Schatzkammern* of Dresden, Munich, Kassel and Vienna. Many of the ruling dynasties in Renaissance Europe had, through inheritance from their medieval predecessors, a residue of rare items – often objects of a devotional or even sacred purpose – and these were gradually incorporated and placed alongside the new treasures. Similarly, leading families, like the Medici and the Hapsburgs, had long collected objects of classical antiquity, many of which are still preserved in the Pitti Palace in Florence and in the Imperial collections in Vienna to this day. Baron Ferdinand acquired, either from his father or through his own efforts, a few fine examples of this type, which merit some discussion before beginning a survey of the Renaissance craftsmanship in the Bequest.

Four Hellenistic bronze medallions found in a tomb near Amisos (present-day Samsun), in the province of Trebizond, on the southern shores of the Black Sea, are the earliest objects in the Bequest. Each has a beautiful head, modelled in very high relief, in the style of the second century BC; on the slightly larger pair the head represents a Bacchante (Figs.3,4), whilst on the second pair one depicts Serapis and the other is Isis.

The problem of where these medallions were made – both Italy and Lower Egypt have been suggested as the most likely locations – is no less difficult to solve than the question of their function. Bronze attachments of this particular size and design, in which the ring is suspended from the lower edge of the medallion, seem rarely to have survived. Consequently, their purpose must remain conjectural, though their relatively weak method of construction makes it improbable that they were intended to take any heavy strain. Large and imposing pieces of furniture, the interior doors of grand buildings and, out-of-doors, the sides of chariots or litters immediately suggest themselves as the most likely objects that, judging from the pictorial and archaeological evidence, were ornamented with such sculptural attachments. Their quality, combined with their rarity, make these four bronzes truly outstanding antiquities from the classical world.

Of the medieval masterpieces in the Bequest, the earliest is the *chasse* or reliquary of Ste Valérie (Colour Pl. IA). It dates from the Late Romanesque period, probably the decade 1170–80, and was made in France at Limoges to contain the relics of Ste Valérie, the daughter of the Roman governor of Aquitaine, whose martyrdom had taken place in Limoges and whose remains had long been preserved and venerated there. The relics of saints, chiefly the bones, were frequently kept in caskets or cases, which were known as reliquaries. One shape that was popular from early medieval times was the miniature church-like form, with its two pointed 'gables' at either end and its 'roof' rising steeply to the apex or ridge running along the length of the casket; the 'roof' was often a hinged lid, though in this instance the entire front of the gable roof is removable and is provided with three locks. In France, this form of reliquary is known as a *chasse*. This reliquary of Ste Valérie is one of the earliest and finest examples of the technique of *champlevé* enamelling on copper produced in Limoges.

The *champlevé* technique requires a thick metal because the design is created by gouging out parts of the surface to create troughs and channels, into which the coloured enamels (in a powdered form) can be placed and, subsequently, fused by heating. The ridges of metal separating the channels and troughs from each other are often part of the outline of the design. On this *chasse*, the range of colours is exceptionally varied, and because most of the remaining surface has been gilded and, on the front, elaborately engraved with scrolls – the so-called *vermiculé* style – the effect is very rich and splendid.

The gifted artist-enameller has decorated the front of the *chasse* with four scenes from the story of the Martyrdom of Ste Valérie, and, at either 'gable' end, he has depicted a full-length angel with a book and a censer (Fig.5). On all these four copper plaques it is only the figures that are enamelled, and so they are seen against a gilded background; in contrast, the beautiful Romanesque ornamental design of the back (Colour Pl. IB), so reminiscent of Spanish enamelling of the twelfth century, is achieved by enamelling the backgrounds and engraving the gilded metal with the figures of animals and with

Fig. 3 Two of the four Hellenistic bronze medallions with ring-handles, found near Amisos, on the southern shores of the Black Sea; probably 2nd century BC. Diam. (of largest medallion) 5⅝ in (14.3 cm).

14

decorative motifs. The high quality of the engraving combined with the excellence of the *champlevé* technique on works of this calibre quickly established the reputation of Limoges as one of the great centres of the art of enamelling in Europe, rivalling the centres in Spain and the valleys of the Rhine and the Meuse.

On the front vertical surface, two episodes of the Martyrdom of Ste Valérie are portrayed with considerable artistic ability: to the left, her fiancé, a young Roman proconsul just returned to Gaul from an expedition, is seen seated on a throne condemning her to death, having discovered that, in his absence, Ste Valérie, the rich and beautiful daughter of the former Roman governor of Aquitaine, has been converted to Christianity by St Martial and has taken the vows of poverty and chastity. On the right, watched by others through an open doorway, the executioner severs the saint's head but, miraculously, it falls into her own hands, while the Hand of God, emerging from a cloud, blesses the scene. On the 'roof', there are two consecutive scenes: on the right, Ste Valérie, aided by an angel, walks forward carrying her severed head until she kneels before the Bishop, St Martial, to whom she offers her head; he turns from the altar, on which the chalice, paten and candle are depicted, and, watched by the deacon, he receives the head of the saint. At the same time, on the left, her fiancé is shown still on his throne but lacking all the previous signs of majesty and

Fig. 4 Head of a Bacchante; a detail of one of the four Hellenistic medallions seen in profile. H. (of relief) 2¼ in (5.7 cm).

command, as he listens to the executioner's account of the miraculous event and then, as foretold by Ste Valérie, he watches the executioner being struck down by an arrow from heaven.

Only one other twelfth-century Limoges enamelled reliquary of Ste Valérie is known; it was presented by Prince Basilewsky to the Hermitage Museum, Leningrad. On both *chasses* the scenes of the Martyrdom of Ste Valérie are so similar that undoubtedly they were made about the same time – certainly in the same decade – and copied from the same sources, perhaps even made in the same workshop. It has been suggested that the reason for the almost simultaneous manufacture (about 1170) of these two very similar *chasses* of Ste Valérie might have been the re-distribution of the relics of both St Martial and Ste Valérie that was taking place between 1160 and 1165, when, for example, three canons sent to Limoges from England by the Bishop of Lincoln were, with the agreement of the authorities in Limoges, permitted to take away in an ivory *chasse* some of the relics. Perhaps it was decided at that time to re-house some of the remaining relics of Ste Valérie, and so these two *chasses* were ordered to be made in the current style using the fashionable technique of *champlevé* enamelling.

Enamelling on glass was an art that was almost unknown in the early fourteenth century in Europe, though gilded and enamelled glasses made at Damascus in Syria and other parts of the Islamic world in the thirteenth and fourteenth centuries were reaching the courts of Western Europe; they were highly prized treasures and a few

Fig. 6 An Islamic lamp of enamelled glass from a mosque, with six suspension loops and a broad band of Arabic lettering; made in Syria, mid-14th century. H. 12 in (30.5 cm).

Fig. 5 (*Right*) A Romanesque gilt copper plaque depicting an angel with book and censer, from a 'gable' end of the Ste Valérie *chasse* (see Colour Pl. 1); *champlevé* enamelling, Limoges, *c*.1170. H. 6½ in (16.5 cm).

16

Fig. 7 The gold enamelled Reliquary of the Holy Thorn, made for Jean de France, duc de Berry, *c*.1405–10 (see Colour Pl. II). H. 12 in (30.5 cm).

Fig. 9 The back of Jean, duc de Berry's Reliquary of the Holy Thorn with the doors of St Michael and St Christopher protecting a second rock-crystal 'window'. French, *c*.1405–10.

examples can still be found in the ancient *Schatzkammern* of the German princes, notably in Dresden and Kassel. In the Waddesdon Bequest, there is a fine Mosque lamp with six glass loops trailed on to the body for suspension (Fig.6). Probably made in Syria in the middle of the fourteenth century, this lamp has ornamental Arabic inscriptions and designs executed in opaque red and blue vitreous enamels, applied cold and fixed to the surface of the clear glass by firing.

The most important Gothic object in the Bequest is the gold enamelled Reliquary of the Holy Thorn (Fig.7), which was made in France probably between 1405 and 1410; until the middle of the nineteenth century it had been kept for at least 200 years within the ecclesiastical treasury of the Austrian Imperial House in the Hofburg of Vienna. This reliquary (Colour Pl. II) was made to house a very special relic – one complete Holy Thorn, 2 in (5 cm) long, that belonged to that rich and powerful French prince, Jean, duc de Berry (1340–1416).

The Crown of Thorns, perhaps the most treasured of the sacred relics preserved by the Byzantine Emperors in their palace at Constantinople, was brought to France in 1239 by Louis IX (Saint Louis), and within the royal palace in Paris, Louis IX built one of the most beautiful Gothic churches ever conceived – the Sainte-Chapelle – to house this and several other holy relics. His successors, however, claimed the privilege of detaching single Thorns from the Crown whenever they wished to make a gift of special importance and, in consequence, there are now a number of reliquaries containing a Thorn, or a part of a Thorn, to be found in treasuries in widely scattered parts of Europe. None, however, can rival the duc de Berry's magnificent creation, which bears his coat of arms – *semée fleurs-de-lis or, within a bordure engrailed gules* – on two small, oblong, gold enamelled plaques set in the gold castellated walls of the base on either side of the portal (Fig. 8).

As a younger son of King Jean II of France, the duc de Berry was politically overshadowed by his three brothers but as a patron of the arts and of learning he was their equal and, in some spheres of patronage, he even excelled them. To his court, for example, he attracted the Limbourg brothers, whose crowning achievement was the incomparable illuminated Book of Hours, known as the *Très Riches Heures* of the duc de Berry. In his own day, the duc's wonderful library was probably no less famous than his collection of masterpieces of goldsmiths' work, most of which were to be melted down shortly after his death in 1416. However, a fair impression can be gained by reading the lengthy lists so painstakingly drawn up by the duc's steward, Robinet d'Estampes; not only does Jean, duc de Berry, emerge as a medieval Maecenas but he also appears to have been a passionate collector, not just of great works of art, precious gems, antique medals and sculptures, but also of curiosities, such as rare plants, fossils, ostrich eggs, unicorns – and, above all, of sacred relics like a piece of the Robe of Our Lord, the milk-tooth of the Virgin Mary and the wedding-ring of St Joseph.

In 1401, the duc de Berry owned a crown of gold set with four Thorns from the Crown of Thorns, according to the Inventory of 1401–3; three of these Thorns he later presented to the chapel of his palace at Bourges, and the fourth Holy Thorn, which he had set '*in uno magno jocali auri*' (in a great gold reliquary), is probably the one that has survived in the Waddesdon Bequest, since this reliquary both dates from the first decade of the fifteenth century and bears the duc de Berry's arms in a discreetly prominent position within the architectural design of the lower part.

The sacred relic was the *raison d'être* of this masterpiece of goldsmiths' work, and, despite the fact that the Holy Thorn is a rather thin and inconspicuous object, the goldsmith has succeeded in making it the focal point of this jewelled shrine by setting it vertically into a large and very eye-catching cabochon sapphire at the very centre of an elaborate construction, all the elements of which form part of one scene – the Last Judgement or Second Coming.

At the apex, God the Father, crowned and holding a sceptre and orb, is seen against a golden glory encircled with pearls and cabochon gems; in front and slightly below, two angels kneel in adoration. There is evidence to show that the Dove (the Holy Spirit) may originally have been attached in the centre at this point. The central part of the Reliquary, which includes the Holy Thorn itself, is protected by a rock-crystal

Fig. 8 Detail of the Resurrection scene and the castellated walls of the Holy Thorn Reliquary, set with the gold enamelled coat of arms of Jean, duc de Berry (died 1416).

'window' and depicts Christ seated on a rainbow with His feet resting on the globe. He displays the sacred Five Wounds, and behind Him, shining in low relief, is the outline of the Cross; above, two angels appear on either side carrying two of the Instruments of the Passion (the nails and the spear) and holding over His head the Crown of Thorns. Below Christ, on either side of the sacred relic, are the kneeling suppliant figures of the Virgin Mary (on the left) and St John the Baptist, the duc's patron saint (on the right). A wide, semi-architectural moulding or frame ornamented with Gothic foliage and set with pearls and cabochon gems encloses this scene within its deep niche and, together with the covering rock-crystal 'window', gives a secluded remoteness to the centre of this shrine. Inside the 'window' is serene majesty and adoring supplication; outside, the twelve gesticulating busts of the Apostles are all expressive of noisy movement and jubilation. All carry their emblems, led by St Peter with his key at the top right-hand side, and all are bearded, except for St John the Divine, whose youthful visage obtrudes in the middle of the left-hand group.

Bridging the gap between this heavenly scene and the Resurrection of the Dead on Earth below is a golden scroll bearing the Latin inscription, written in black enamel:

ISTA EST UNA SPINA CORONE

DOMINI NOSTRI IHESU XPISTI

(This is a thorn from the crown of Our Lord Jesus Christ.)

This elaborate and complex representation of the Last Judgement has been created by fashioning the gold and applying enamel by a new technique, often referred to as 'enamelling in the round' (*émail en ronde bosse* is the French term). French goldsmiths working at the courts of Charles VI and his uncle, the duc de Berry, created out of thin sheets of gold these small-scale sculptures either in the round or in very high relief; on to the modelled surfaces, they skilfully fused both opaque and translucent enamels and, on to the opaque white enamel, they even applied coloured enamels, as, for example, on the feathered wings of the two angels attending Christ in Majesty. This brilliant technical achievement enabled the goldsmith for the first time to create on a three-dimensional scale the illusion of human flesh and clothing, natural foliage and floral beauty. One documented example, now lost but fortunately recorded in an eighteenth-century painting, represents St Michael slaying the Dragon and was made, apparently, with a similar kind of base composed of an enamelled grassy mound within an encircling castellated wall of gold; this piece is known to have been pawned by King Charles VI of France in 1404. Indeed, a similar fate befell the finest of the group – the *Goldenes Rössel* (preserved in the treasury of the pilgrimage church of Altötting, near Munich). It was a New Year's Day present to Charles VI of France from his wife in 1404 but, in the following year, the King gave it to the Queen's brother, Ludwig of Bavaria, in lieu of a year's pension that the King owed him; Ludwig's heirs presented it to the church of Altötting in 1509 and so the *Goldenes Rössel* escaped the melting-pot into which so many of the French royal treasures disappeared. No doubt, the Holy Thorn Reliquary in the Waddesdon Bequest escaped for a similar reason, but that part of its history has still to be traced.

The flat back of the Holy Thorn Reliquary (Fig.9) was originally richly decorated with translucent enamelling, particularly the areas of the two reliefs on the gold doors depicting St Michael and St Christopher. Having suffered some damage, all the remaining traces of enamel were apparently removed with meticulous care in the middle of the nineteenth century in an attempt to give an unimpaired appearance to

Fig. 10 Detail of the doors of the Holy Thorn Reliquary, showing the stippled or pounced decoration, especially the feathered wings of St Michael, the halo of the Christ Child, and the floral motifs on the backgrounds and on the draperies.

this great jewel. In the process of cleaning away the enamel, the surface of the gold has been rubbed and smoothed down; consequently, the delicate stipple or pounced decoration, which was designed to be seen through the layer of translucent coloured enamel, has become very faint and only when the light falls on the surface at a certain angle can its full extent and extraordinary *finesse* be appreciated (Fig. 10). Apart from pounced designs covering the draperies, complete pictorial elements – such as the wings of St Michael – are executed entirely in this technique of stippling and the minute dots are so skilfully pounced that a three-dimensional visual effect is created. This form of decoration is rare but in the late fourteenth century, especially among the goldsmiths working at the French courts, the skill was developed into an art-form of the greatest subtlety.

The style of the two figures on the gold doors with their rather exaggerated, mannered, Gothic elegance was already evolving in France under Charles V (died 1380), the brother of Jean, duc de Berry, and in its earlier and less 'sweet' form, this figure style can be seen in the reliefs on one of the major surviving pieces of goldsmiths' work from that reign, the sceptre of Charles V (preserved in the Louvre). The two doors of this reliquary are, however, masterpieces of that 'soft' decorative elegance which dominated Gothic art almost everywhere in Europe around 1400, both north and south of the Alps, and has led to this style being known as the 'International Gothic'.

The golden doors open to reveal a rock-crystal window, similar in size to the one on the front. The area behind it is no longer in its original state, and it is a matter of surmise what was kept in the shallow space behind the rock-crystal – perhaps another relic, such as a fragment of the Robe of Christ, or perhaps a signed statement authenticating the Relic of the Holy Thorn. The choice of the two saints, St Michael and St Christopher, for the decoration of the doors is curious and as yet unexplained but may have been dictated by the particular object preserved behind the rock-crystal window. An equally puzzling feature of the back of this reliquary is the small semicircular niche in the castellated architecture of the base; in its present state it serves no purpose and yet it is most unconvincing as a purely decorative feature. Its function may, however, have been related to the lost central element of the architectural base, which is only indicated by the sheared-off edges of the gold floor of the niche and of the gold arches below. The altered state of the back of this great jewelled reliquary poses several intriguing questions, but unfortunately neither the earliest mention of this reliquary in the Inventory of the Geichliche Schatzkammer at Vienna in 1677 nor any of the subsequent descriptions supply the answers.

The other medieval works of art in the Bequest belong to the Late Gothic era in Northern Europe, spanning the last few decades of the fifteenth and the first quarter of the sixteenth centuries. In the main, these creations of the metalworker and the wood-carver reflect the transition from the Gothic to the full-scale adoption of the Italian Renaissance style north of the Alps.

Of the two large wooden sculptures, the finer is the figure of St Catherine trampling underfoot the Emperor Maximian (Figs. 11, 12), though the slightly earlier figure of St George typifies the German Late Gothic 'sweet' style. The restored polychrome St George figure was probably carved in Southern Germany towards the end of the fifteenth century when a particularly soft mannered style continued to characterise much of the sculpture emanating from those workshops. In marked contrast, the St Catherine, which was carved in the vicinity of Maastricht in the early sixteenth

23

24

Fig. 11 (*Far left*) St Catherine of Alexander; wood, perhaps originally polychrome. The Saint's left hand is restored. Attributed to Jan van Steffeswert, working in the Meuse region, *c.* 1500–25. H. 36 in (91.4 cm).

Fig. 12 (*Left*) The back of the St Catherine figure with its well-carved details, revealing the strength of the last phase of the Flemish Gothic tradition, in which the sculptor had been trained.

Fig. 13 (*Above*) A detail from the St Catherine figure: the Roman Emperor Maximian (AD 286–305) expressively depicted in a vanquished pose.

century, has more character and, in particular, the expressive treatment of the prostrate Emperor Maximian (Fig. 13) is an example of the high artistic level that was being achieved in certain workshops in the Meuse region (near Aachen) at this period. Indeed, the Waddesdon St Catherine is now confidently attributed to the workshop of the talented sculptor Jan van Steffeswert, who was active in and around Maastricht from 1501 to 1524 and whose figure of St Barbara at Neeroeteren is closely similar in many respects. Few of his works have survived, and in England the only other sculpture from the hand of Jan van Steffeswert known to exist is the Virgin of the Crescent in St Mary's College, Oscott.

The other examples of late medieval wood-carving in the Bequest, although made not far away in the Southern Netherlands, are of a totally different character; they are

Fig. 15 (*Right*) A detail of the miniature tabernacle (see Fig. 14), showing the central spherical section fully opened. L. 5 in (12.7 cm).

Fig. 14 (*Far left*) Miniature tabernacle of boxwood; each of the three main sections is detachable and designed to open, revealing further minutely carved scenes from the Life and Passion of Christ. Southern Netherlands, first quarter of 16th century. H. 8¾ in (22.2 cm).

Fig. 16 (*Left*) Outer case for the miniature tabernacle (see Fig. 14), made of treated leather (*cuir bouilli*), decorated with foliate ornament and heraldic badges and coats of arms indicating that it had belonged to the Emperor Charles v (1519–56). Southern Netherlands, first quarter of 16th century; the gold filigree mounts, openwork hinges and the lock were probably added in Spain at a slightly later date. H. 10¼ in (26 cm).

all microscopic sculptures, each a veritable masterpiece of virtuoso wood-carving. Made for private devotion and personal enjoyment, these miniature boxwood carvings were among the treasured possessions of some of the most illustrious figures at the courts of Northern Europe, including the Emperor Maximilian I's daughter, Margaret of Austria (1480–1530), who was Regent of the Netherlands. In England, King Henry VIII and his Queen, Catherine of Aragon, owned the rosary which is now preserved among the Duke of Devonshire's collections at Chatsworth. Nearly 2 ft (60 cm) long, this rosary is complete and bears the English royal arms together with the initials of their Majesties and must, therefore, date from after their marriage in 1509 and before the divorce proceedings had begun in 1527, or, at the latest, before 1533 when the marriage was declared null and void and Catherine was deprived of her title of Queen.

One of the most brilliant and ambitious creations of this group, an elaborate tabernacle, is in the Bequest (Fig.14), and there are convincing indications that it may have belonged to the Emperor Charles V (1519–56). The incredible dexterity, patience and artistic ability of the carver, working on so minute a scale and creating such extraordinarily crowded figure scenes in a three-dimensional form, cannot but excite wonder and amazement. Unfortunately, nothing is known about the workshops in which they were made, though they appear to have been located somewhere in the Southern Netherlands, probably at Antwerp, Malines or Brussels; the head of the main workshop may have been the author of the one signed piece so far discovered – a rosary bead in the Fine Arts Museum, Copenhagen, with the inscription ADAM THEODRICI ME FECIT ('Adam Theodrici made me'). Significantly, all the carvings in this group seem to have been made within a short period, certainly less than fifty years, at the end of the fifteenth and during the first few decades of the sixteenth centuries.

Most of the surviving pieces are beads from rosaries – there are four in the Waddesdon Bequest – and these hinged spherical objects open up to reveal minutely carved biblical scenes inside, occasionally protected by miniature 'doors' decorated with scenes carved in low relief. The miniature altar-piece (Fig.17), engraved with the date 1511, is probably one of the most splendid examples to have survived and certainly is most unusual for not being wholly Gothic in every detail – the use of two pairs of wrestling 'putti' on the base and of pilaster-type decoration on the side panels of the base, for example, are rare instances in the work of this master of an awareness of the influence of the Renaissance. In the wholly Gothic tabernacle (Fig.14), however, this master's technical virtuosity can be seen in its most ambitious form. The object is so ingeniously constructed that, like a flower, it opens, and, section by section, reveals more and yet more areas of minute carving depicting scenes from the life of Christ. The process commences when the finial, a pelican in her piety, is lifted off and the four 'petals' below open outwards to reveal, carved on their inner faces, scenes of events surrounding Christ's birth and in the centre, carved fully in the round, the figure of the Virgin and Child, which simultaneously rises as the wooden ratchet (at the base of the pinnacle) is slowly turned. Similarly, the central 'knop' of the tabernacle opens up like a rosary bead (Fig.15) and the stem, with its fine tracery, is designed to be taken apart. An object of such exquisite workmanship and inventiveness would, undoubtedly, have been the cherished object of piety in some private oratory of a royal household. Although its outer leather case has the armorial bearings of the Emperor Charles V, who retired to a monastery in Spain and died there in 1558, and the object was stated (as early as 1834) to have been brought to England from Spain during the Peninsular

Fig. 17 Miniature altarpiece of
boxwood, dated 1511, fitted with
two tiny compartments, perhaps
for relics. In design, it closely
resembles the great monumental
altarpieces of contemporary
Netherlandish sculptors.
H. 9⅞ in (25.1 cm).

Fig. 18 Book-cover of Ulm
Münster (companion to Colour
Pl. III). Silver, partly gilt and
with enamelled shields, the
central roundel is modern,
perhaps replacing a circular
rock-crystal reliquary. Ulm,
1506. H. 11⅜ in (28.9 cm).

War (1808–14), this distinguished provenance has yet to be established beyond doubt (Fig. 16).

Of the few items of Late Gothic metalwork in the Bequest, the most important are the so-called 'Bamberg book-covers' (Colour Pl. III, Fig. 18), which are now known to have been made at Ulm, in Southern Germany, in 1506 for its great Gothic Münster. Bearing neither a town mark nor a maker's mark, these silver covers of a book of the Gospels had been associated with the cathedral City of Bamberg because an inscription scratched on the back states that they were sold in 1803 from the religious foundation dedicated to St Stephen in Bamberg. The former attribution of these masterpieces of Late Gothic goldsmiths' work to Thomas Rockenbach, the Bamberg goldsmith who in 1485–6 made the silver-gilt monstrance of the Holy Nail, which is still to be seen in the Treasury of Bamberg Cathedral, and the more recent thesis that these covers were made in nearby Nuremberg about 1518 have both recently been disproved.

The arms on the two shields attached to both of the book-covers had not previously been recognised, but as a result of my identification of the arms as those of the Münster of Ulm and of the City of Ulm, searches began in the German archives. References to the book-covers were found and subsequently published by Dr J. M. Fritz; they not only confirmed the fact that the book-covers had been made for the Münster in Ulm but also shed light on their later history, including their lucky removal to the Benedictine Abbey at Elchingen, where they remained until 1785. For that reason, these book-covers escaped the fate that befell most of the goldsmiths' work and precious treasures of Ulm and its Münster and, because of their quality and excellent state of preservation, they eventually came to rest in Baron Anselm's collection in Vienna.

The rear book-cover (Fig. 18) has the symbols of the four Evangelists in the roundels at the corners and, in the deep niches on either side, the standing figures of St Anthony (on the left) and a canonised deacon, probably St Lawrence (on the right). In the centre, there is a modern silver boss replacing, no doubt, a circular rock-crystal reliquary, over which the two flying angels would have held a crown.

The front book-cover (Colour Pl. III) is, however, complete; in the centre, the beautiful group of the Virgin and Child, attended by two angels holding her cloak and two more above holding a crown over her head, is gilded. In the niches on either side are the finely modelled figures of St Helena with the True Cross (on the right) and a bishop with a cripple at his feet (perhaps St John the Almoner); in the corners are four of the Fathers of the Church (St Jerome, St Ambrose, St Gregory and St Augustine).

A silver book-cover of similar design is preserved among the insignia and regalia of the Holy Roman Empire in the Hofburg in Vienna; it was made by Hans von Reutlingen in Aachen towards the end of the fifteenth century. However, the later and more developed style of the Ulm Münster book-covers is evident in the greater sense of three-dimensional spatial effects and of whimsical playfulness in the treatment of the elaborate tracery and the curving pinnacles. The sophisticated treatment of the beautiful figure group of the Virgin and Child is masterly and contrasts with the heavier style of the figures on Hans von Reutlingen's work. These book-covers are rare examples of the art of the goldsmith in the very last and most exuberant phase of the Late Gothic style, echoing the achievements of sculptors and architects in Southern German cities.

The fascination of natural phenomena in its more unusual manifestations led the courts of Europe to collect beautiful coloured and veined hard-stones (like chalcedony, agate, aquamarine, jasper, bloodstone, amethyst, garnet, etc). When polished on the wheel and fashioned into elegant or eccentric forms, these hard-stones would be trimmed with gold or silver mounts, often enriched with gem-stones and enamelled ornament. This fashion was to be given enormous impetus by such arbiters of taste as Isabella d'Este at Mantua, who died in 1539, and by the example of the Medici in Florence; but already in the fifteenth century many court treasuries, even north of the Alps, contained handsome examples, though the few that have survived today would seem to indicate that traditional shapes and simple forms of surface decoration were preferred in the period around 1500. In the Bequest, a chalcedony cup and cover (Colour Pl. IV) in the Late Gothic style has been ornamented with simple gadrooning (spiral fluting), executed on the lathe and finely polished. The discreet silver-gilt mounts are an integral part of the design and in no way distract from the soft colouring of the stone, which passes from grey through lilac to a milky white, occasionally veined with streaks of red and white.

Such bizarre effects of banded colour in minerals clearly fired the imagination of the Venetian glassmakers, who in the fifteenth century were on the threshold of capturing the European market. In 1500, when Marcantonio Coccio Sabellico published his *Opera Omnia*, he wrote (in Book III, *De Venetae urbis situ*) that the Venetian glassmakers 'began to turn the materials into various colours and numberless forms . . . there is no kind of precious stone which cannot be imitated by the industry of the glass workers, a sweet contest of nature and of man'.

The Bequest, which contains several later rock-crystal and other hard-stone cups, has three of the rarest Venetian glasses designed to rival the qualities of these natural stones. These masterpieces of the Venetian glassmaker are discussed in Chapter 3; in their use of the Late Gothic shapes popular in the silver plate made north of the Alps, the Venetian glassmakers of the Early Renaissance reveal the strength of the Gothic tradition in Northern Italy as late as 1500.

PLATE IA. THE STE VALÉRIE CHASSE, Limoges, France, *c*. 1170. L. 11½ in (29.2 cm).

This miniature church-like casket was made to contain the relics of the Saint, and the scenes in *champlevé* enamelling on copper (on the front) are from the story of her Martyrdom in 3rd-century Gaul and are portrayed in the Late Romanesque style.

PLATE IB. *Detail of the back of the Chasse* showing a very different effect obtained by reversing the technique so that the enamelling is restricted entirely to the backgrounds and the animals and other decorative motifs are finely engraved on the gilded metal. H. 6½ in (16.5 cm).

PLATE II. THE HOLY THORN RELIQUARY OF JEAN, DUC DE BERRY, French, *c.* 1405–10.

This detail focuses on the central part of the Last Judgement scene, a miniature work of Gothic sculpture fashioned in gold and enriched with enamel, sapphire, spinels and pearls. Set in the centre is the Holy Thorn itself, taken from the Crown of Thorns so triumphantly brought from Constantinople to Paris in 1239 by King Louis IX (St Louis).

PLATE III. THE ULM MÜNSTER BOOK-COVER, German, 1506. H. 11½ in (29.2 cm).

One of a pair of covers (see Fig.18), made of silver and partially gilded; the shields of arms are enamelled. Both the exuberance of the architectural forms and the sophisticated style of the figure are masterly expressions of that very last phase of the Late Gothic in Southern Germany, which was soon to be eclipsed by the all-pervasive influence of the Italian Renaissance.

PLATE IV. A CHALCEDONY CUP AND COVER, exemplifying the courtly taste in the Late Gothic period for collecting beautiful veined hard-stones, shaped and polished on the wheel; mounted in silver-gilt oak leaves and other naturalistic motifs of simple design. H. 10½ in (26.7 cm).

PLATE V. THE DEBLÍN COVERED STANDING-CUP, Venice, 15th century. H. 17½ in (44.5 cm).

This early example of Venetian *cristallo* glass is both gilded and enamelled in characteristic manner but, most exceptionally, has applied bosses of coloured glass. Furthermore, the diamond-engraved inscription (on the foot) is in Czech and refers to the Lords of Deblín, whose castle and lands were near Brno in Bohemia.

Plate VIA (*Right*). GLASS GOBLET, Venice, late 15th century.
H. 7 in (17.8 cm).

One of three surviving specimens of this curious turquoise-blue
glass made in imitation of the semi-precious stone; this goblet is
also remarkable for the superiority of its enamelled figure
drawing.

Plate VIB (*Below*). GLASS BEAKER AND COVER, Venice or *façon
de Venise*, 17th century. H. 9¼ in (23.5 cm).

This 'opal' (or *girasol*) glass was yet another of the Venetian
glassmakers' successful imitations of precious stones.

Plate VII (*Right*). MAIOLICA VASE, from the workshop of Orazio
Fontana in Urbino, *c.*1565–70. H. 21½ in (54.6 cm).

This signed work is one of a pair of vases, which had already been fitted
with French *ormolu* mounts of neo-classical design when Horace Walpole
purchased them in Paris in 1765–6.

PLATE VIII. 'DIDO AND AENEAS', Limoges painted enamel plaque, *c.* 1530–40. H. 8¾ in (22.2 cm).

This scene of Aeneas leaving Carthage is copied from a woodcut illustration in an edition of Virgil's *Opera* first printed in 1502 (see Fig.22).

PLATE IXA. PORTRAIT OF A YOUNG NOBLEMAN, painted enamel plaque signed by Léonard Limosin and dated 1550. Diam. 3¾ in (9.5 cm).

Léonard Limosin, a talented enameller from Limoges, worked at Fontainebleau for François I (died 1547) and for Henri II, who appointed him '*valet de chambre du Roy*' in 1548.

PLATE IXB. 'APOLLO ON MOUNT HELICON', Limoges painted enamel dish signed by Susanne Court, late 16th century. L. 19½ in (49.5 cm).

Copied from an engraving by Giorgio Ghisi of Mantua, this subject was extremely popular, perhaps because of its relevance to the Renaissance garden with its emphasis on rocks, water, grottoes and music.

PLATE XA. THREE CONTINENTAL JEWELS OF THE SIXTEENTH CENTURY

A toothpick, in the form of a mermaid with a body formed of a baroque pearl set in enamelled gold. L. $3\frac{1}{10}$ in (8 cm).

'The Conversion of St Paul', a gold enamelled repoussé scene set with diamonds and rubies, designed to be worn by a man as a hat jewel. Diam. $1\frac{7}{8}$ in (4.8 cm).

'Charity', a pendant jewel set with emeralds and diamonds, in the style of Erasmus Hornick's designs published in Nuremberg in 1565. L. with ring $3\frac{3}{4}$ in (9.4 cm).

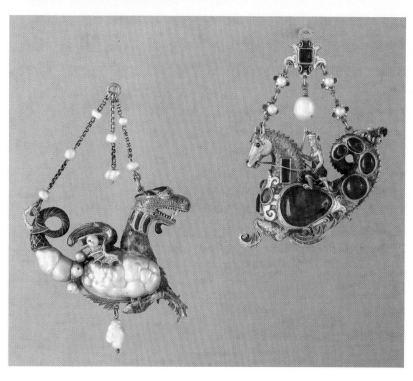

PLATE XB. TWO SPANISH RENAISSANCE JEWELS

Sea-dragon pendant, composed of two baroque pearls set in enamelled gold. L. $3\frac{7}{8}$ in (9.8 cm).

Hippocamp pendant, enamelled gold set with emeralds, probably brought from the New World, perhaps from the Columbian mines. L. $3\frac{3}{8}$ in (8.6 cm).

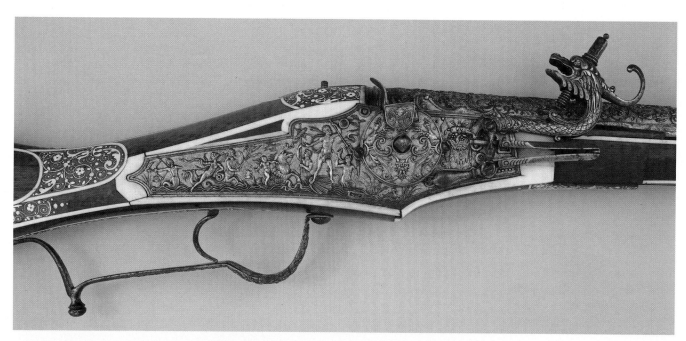

PLATE XIIA (*Left*). DETAIL OF THE LOCK-PLATE OF A GUN, by Daniel Sadeler, made for the court of Maximilian I, Duke of Bavaria, *c*.1620 (see Figs.63,64 for two views of the gun).

PLATE XIIB (*Left, below*). A SHIELD OF PARADE, signed by Giorgio Ghisi of Mantua and dated 1554. Diam. 22 in (55.9 cm).

In the hands of this Italian master, the art of damascening on iron with gold and silver has been combined with the new language of Italian Mannerist ornament and art.

PLATE XIIIA (*Right*). A HAND-BELL, by Wenzel Jamnitzer, *c*.1555–60. H. 5¼ in (13.3 cm).

All the little lizards, insects and flowers are cast from life in silver and, it is said, no chiselled work or chasing was subsequently carried out to achieve their realistic finish.

PLATE XIIIB (*Below*). THREE NATURAL CURIOSITIES SET IN SILVER-GILT MOUNTS

A nut from the Seychelles (in the Indian Ocean) in mid-16th-century German mounts. H. 16 in (40.6 cm).

A nautilus shell in Antwerp mounts of 1555–6. H. 9 in (22.9 cm).

An ostrich egg in Prague mounts of the late 16th century. H. 15¼ in (38.7 cm).

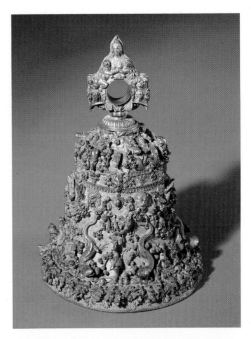

Plate xiva. The grape-picker, by Elias
Lencker, of Nuremberg, 1562–91.
H. 8¾ in (22.2 cm).

Few comparable works of sculpture in silver have
survived.

Plate xivb. Casket, with Limoges painted
enamel panels by the 'Master k.i.p.' and
silver-gilt mounts, French, c. 1535.
L. 5¾ in (14.6 cm).

Plate xv. Four silver-gilt
standing-cups from Nuremberg

The Cup with the Pope, by
Michael Müller, c.1620. H. 19 in
(48.3 cm).

The *Traubenpokal* ('bunch of
grapes cup') by Hans Petzolt,
c.1600. H. 25¼ in (64.1 cm).

The Cup with the Cupid, by
Jacob Stoer, second quarter of
17th century. H. 14¾ in (37.5 cm).

The Cup with a rider, by Hans
Petzolt, late 16th century.
H. 22 in (55.9 cm).

PLATE XVIA. SILVER-GILT STANDING-CUP AND COVER, set with French shell cameos of early 16th century; perhaps made in Strasburg *c*.1520–30. H. 11½ in (29.2 cm).

AMBER TANKARD, carved with the Vices and the royal arms of Sweden, made at Königsberg (on the Baltic coast). *c*.1650–60. H. 8 in (20.3 cm).

PLATE XVIB. *Detail of the amber tankard*, with its fine carving in low relief; attributed to Jacob Heise, who signed a similar piece in the Grünes Gewölbe, Dresden.

3. Glass of the Renaissance

In fifteenth-century Italy, the great mercantile centre that handled so much of Europe's trade with the Orient was Venice. Under the protection of its naval power, its merchant ships plied their trade throughout the Eastern Mediterranean, and close contact with the Islamic world led, no doubt, to Venetian craftsmen acquiring and rivalling certain of these Middle Eastern skills, such as gilding and enamelling on glass. Although the glass industry of Venice had existed long before 1271, when the first written rules for the Venetian guild of glassmakers were approved, it was apparently not until about 1450–70 that the Venetians discovered the secret of producing a clear, colourless glass; they gave it the name *cristallo*, for they could at last rival the purity of rock-crystal. At about the same time they seem to have perfected new varieties of coloured glass for vessels and also the technique of applying enamelled and gilded decoration to the surface of the glass vessels, both *cristallo* and coloured.

In the Bequest, there are two very rare examples, both masterpieces of these newly acquired skills. The more spectacular is a tall standing-cup and cover (Colour Pl. v), the shape of which is wholly Gothic. The wide band of gilding around the rim of the cup with its dotted design of coloured enamels superimposed gives a 'jewelled' effect – a form of ornamentation that became a feature of the finest enamelled glasses from Venice in the late fifteenth and early sixteenth centuries. The rest of the decoration on the sides of the cup is, however, most unexpected: on to the clear glass have been trailed ribs of clear glass, which were subsequently gilded; these ribs have been made to form a loose, lozenge-like pattern and within each of these roughly formed lozenges is applied a blob of coloured glass. These blobs, or 'prunts' as they are usually called, form three horizontal zones, the upper and lower being made of blue and the central being an aubergine or deep red; the tip in the middle of each prunt is gilded.

In Venice the use of 'prunts' as a form of decoration for glass vessels was most exceptional; indeed, only four other examples of this type are known. It seems possible, therefore, that these five magnificent glasses may have been specially made to order for princes or powerful patrons north of the Alps, where such decoration was popular and where the late medieval forest glass-houses, especially in Germany and Bohemia, had a well-established tradition of embellishing their crude greenish glasses with 'prunts'. This interpretation is supported by an inscription, engraved with a diamond on the cover of one of the four similar glasses: it lists four members of the prominent family of von Puckheim and is dated 1639, the year when Count Adolf von Puckheim was killed in a tournament in Prague. Yet more support may be found in the words of the diamond-engraved inscription that has been added to the foot of the Waddesdon Bequest standing-cup; it is written in Czech and may be translated: 'Praise the Lord and drink cool wine to the health of the Lords of Deblín'. The castle of Deblín, with its village and lands, was situated in Bohemia near Brno and, in 1415, passed into the hands of a new overlord, Arkleb z Drahotouše. The Waddesdon glass standing-cup

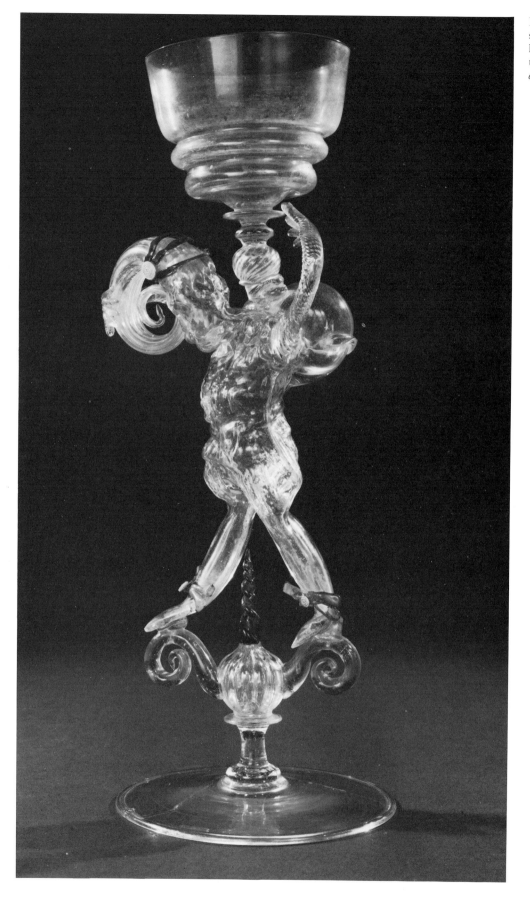

Fig. 19 Drinking-glass with the stem blown to form a hunchback; made of *cristallo* and trimmed with blue glass. Venice, *c.* 1600. H. 12 in (30.5 cm).

and cover, which was most probably made in Venice during the second half of the fifteenth century, does resemble in general shape certain contemporary silver cups from Bohemia and Hungary; it therefore remains an interesting possibility that, after its arrival from Venice, this magnificent tall cup and cover may have become the 'Welcome' cup of the Castle of Deblín.

The other glass in the Bequest, which is perhaps of even greater rarity, is also a graceful Gothic shape (Colour Pl. VIA). It is made of a most curious opaque turquoise-blue glass, of which only two other late-fifteenth-century examples are known. Of the three examples, only two have enamelled figure decoration – the Fairfax Cup (in the Victoria and Albert Museum) and this goblet in the Waddesdon Bequest. As the enamelled scene of Pyramus and Thisbe on the Fairfax Cup is executed in a far more clumsy and primitive style, it has been suggested that the Waddesdon Bequest goblet was painted some decades after the Fairfax Cup. Certainly, the delicacy with which the pairs of lovers in the two roundels on either side of the bowl have been painted is most accomplished, and their costume suggests a date around 1500. The other curious feature about the Waddesdon goblet is that the Venetian glassmaker has achieved a solid hard-stone effect with the turquoise-blue material for, whereas the Fairfax Cup changes to a deep amethyst-red colour by transmitted light, the Waddesdon goblet remains, as intended, opaque like the semi-precious stone it was striving to imitate. Furthermore, the maker of the Waddesdon goblet has skilfully introduced glass of two other colours: a rare lapis-lazuli blue glass for the stem and a brilliant opaque-white for the three bands. As neither the Fairfax Cup nor the other turquoise-blue glass has any such elaborations, this goblet would seem to be the *chef-d'œuvre* of a leading glass-house on the island of Murano in the Venetian lagoon towards the end of the fifteenth century and to represent the sophisticated heights to which the Venetian glassmakers aspired but only rarely attained.

By the early sixteenth century, the virtuosity and manipulative skills of the glass-makers of Murano had become a byword. When the Emperor's son, Archduke Ferdinand (1520–95), set up a glass-house in the grounds of his palace of Ambras, near Innsbruck, in 1563 as his own personal plaything, he obtained the consent of the Council of Ten in Venice to man it with glassblowers from Murano, each chosen because he had the most 'fantasy in him'. This reputation is confirmed by an eye-witness account written in 1550 by Georgius Agricola (1490–1555) in his *De Re Metallico* (Book XII); it reads:

Glassmen make a variety of objects: cups, phials, pitchers, globular bottles, dishes, saucers, mirrors, animals, trees, ships. Of so many fine and wonderful objects I should take long to tell. I have seen such at Venice, and especially at the Feast of the Ascension when they were on sale at Murano, where are the most famous of all glass factories. These I have seen on several occasions, but especially when for certain reasons, I went to meet Andreas Naugerius at his house there, in company with Franciscus Asulanus . . .

A sixteenth-century *cristallo* drinking-glass, with a most unusual stem ingeniously blown in the form of a hunchback (Fig.19), exemplifies the talented creativity of the Venetian glassmakers of the Late Renaissance and, at the same time, highlights an inherent weakness of some of their glass – the tendency to 'crizzle' or 'weep'. This harmful phenomenon, which manifests itself in sticky beads of moisture on the surface of the glass and a network of minute hair cracks spreading throughout the thickness of the glass, can only be arrested – not cured – by keeping the glass in a stable atmosphere where the relative humidity is not allowed to fluctuate. Consequently, this beautiful drinking-glass has to be exhibited within a separate perspex case of its own and a constant relative humidity carefully maintained.

Another stone that presented a difficult challenge to the glassmakers of Murano was the opal. Antonio Neri, in his great textbook *L'Arte Vetraria* (Florence, 1612), mentions among the various precious stones being imitated in glass both opal and *girasol*. In Early Italian, *girasol* was the name given to a milky precious stone, which with transmitted light turned a reddish fiery tint, rather like an opal; hence *girasol* was also the name for a sunflower. It is not easy to recognise opal glass of the Renaissance, especially as so little seems to have survived, but, fortunately, two 'opal' flasks with silver-gilt mounts are preserved in Dresden in the Grünes Gewölbe, where the Saxon royal collections have been housed for centuries. One of the two has the enamelled arms of the Abbot of Kempten (1571–84) and is dated 1574. Both flasks have imperfections, such as the pronounced series of streaks of differing tone, and it is significant that these 'opal' flasks are not quite the same as the 'opal' glasses preserved in Rosenborg Castle, which were acquired in Venice by King Frederick IV of Denmark in 1708–9 and which are consistently described in Danish royal archives as '*vetri di girasol*'.

In the Waddesdon Bequest, an 'opal' or, more correctly, a *girasol* glass beaker and cover (Colour Pl. VIB), made in a three-part mould, has a continuous 'frieze' depicting in relief marine subjects, possibly taken from a Triumph of Neptune. The sea-nymphs and Tritons, together with sea-horses, emerge above the waves and, on the cover, three dolphins radiate outwards from the 'button-knop'. Only eight or nine beakers made from this mould have survived; one of these glasses, an 'opal' version of almost identical quality in the Schloss Pilnitz, Dresden, was evidently mounted in silver gilt before 1732, as it was described with its precious mounts when listed in the Inventory of 1732. However, as its cover of 'opal' glass was quite different, being ribbed, high-domed and lacking the three dolphins, it may not be original. Fortunately, a clear glass beaker from this mould, complete with its cover of the 'triple-dolphin' design, has been preserved in the Kunstindustrie Museum, Copenhagen, and thus helps to confirm that the Waddesdon Bequest beaker has its original cover.

The origin of this extraordinary group of beakers blown in the same three-part mould is uncertain, but they seem to date from the seventeenth century and, although they may be Venetian, the presence of three bun-feet on the clear-glass versions is indicative of a Northern European, perhaps German, taste. Consequently, these rare glasses might have been made in Venice for export to Germany or in one of the glass-houses north of the Alps which were producing glass *façon de Venise*, often with the benefit of skilled Venetian glassblowers who had deserted from Murano to seek their fortune abroad.

4. Italian Maiolica

Just as the technique of enamelled painting on Renaissance glass gradually reached a high level in Venice by the sixteenth century, so likewise the technique of treating earthenware dishes and vessels as 'canvases', on which to paint pictures in many colours, was developed for the first time in Europe by the potters of Renaissance Italy. In the decades around 1500, several potteries in Tuscany, Umbria, the Duchy of Urbino and the small town of Faenza (between Bologna and Rimini) became increasingly proficient in making this new type of pottery, which in contemporary accounts is called *maiolica* or *maiolicha*. Its distinguishing feature was the use of a tin-glaze to coat the reddish earthenware body; the opaque whiteness and smooth even surface created by a well-produced and competently fired tin-glaze provided the ideal base on which to paint in colours. Although the range of pigments available to the maiolica-painter was at first very restricted, almost every colour, except scarlet, was being produced long before the middle of the sixteenth century by successfully blending the different metallic oxides. Once fired in the kiln, these colours never fade; furthermore, these fired colours have special chromatic qualities that give maiolica a distinctive character, which evidently appealed to the leading noble families of Renaissance Italy. Under the patronage of the local ruling family, these potteries attracted the services of painters of considerable merit, who, copying from engravings after the great masters, produced a great variety of figural scenes, mainly derived from classical mythology; this type of maiolica is usually referred to as *istoriato* ware.

In the Waddesdon Bequest, there are several very large, richly painted and incredibly competently fired items of maiolica from Urbino, of which the most important are undoubtedly the two monumental vases (Colour Pl. VII), almost 2 ft (60 cm) high, one of which is inscribed around the sides of the foot: FATE.IN.BOTEGA.DE.ORATIO. FONTANA. (made in the workshop of Orazio Fontana). Orazio's father, Guido Durantino, was the leading *istoriato* painter in Urbino by about 1530, and Orazio, who died in 1571, at the age of sixty-one, worked in the increasingly prosperous and highly esteemed family pottery. According to Vasari in the second edition of his *Vite* (published in Florence in 1568), Guidobaldo II, Duke of Urbino, 'made Battista Franco do a large number of drawings which, when executed in that, the finest earthenware in all Italy, turned out marvellously well. Such great quantities of these vessels were therefore made and of so many kinds, that they would have sufficed for and done honour to a royal service: and the paintings on them would not have been better had they been alone in oils by the finest artists. . . . Duke Guidobaldo sent a double service of this ware to the Emperor Charles V and a service to Cardinal Farnese, brother of Signora Vittoria, his consort'.

A strong case has been made by modern scholars for assuming that much of the best-quality Urbino ware was made in the Fontana family pottery in Urbino, using the designs supplied by court artists, like Battista Franco (*c.* 1510–61), who was a leading

Fig. 20 Italian maiolica bottle, painted with the device and motto used by the Duke of Ferrara on the occasion of his marriage to Margarita Gonzaga. Probably made in Urbino, 1579. H. 15½ in (39.4 cm).

Fig. 21 Italian maiolica bottle, painted with the arms of the sixth Count of Lemos (1548–1601). Probably made in Urbino, 1575, the year of the Count's embassy to Pope Gregory XIII. H. 15⅜ in (39.1 cm).

Mannerist painter and was certainly working for the Duke between about 1545 and 1551. By about 1560, the fame of the Fontana workshop and their large-scale vases and luxury wares, with their ambitious *istoriato* paintings covering the entire surfaces, earned them the patronage of princes further afield. In 1563 Orazio was called to the court of the Duke of Savoy, and after two years in Turin he was able to return to Urbino and open his own establishment in a property in the Borgo San Paolo. In 1567 he was supplying the Cardinal of Urbino with a service for presentation to the powerful Cardinal Alessandro Farnese in Rome. Clearly, he strove to maintain the high standards of earlier *istoriato* painting in his own workshop, but few signed, dated or inscribed pieces have survived. Consequently, this documentary pair of monumental vases in the Bequest, which were probably made soon after 1565, testify to the technical and artistic skill of his workshop at this mature stage in the story of Renaissance maiolica.

Furthermore, this pair of vases are most exceptional in having been enriched during the eighteenth century with specially designed French *ormolu* (gilt-bronze) mounts of high quality. Whilst it had become fashionable in mid-eighteenth-century Paris to mount porcelain, both Oriental and European, in elaborate *ormolu* mounts, there is little evidence to show that maiolica was often treated in this decorative way, and yet, when these two vases were purchased by Horace Walpole during his visit to Paris in 1765–6, he described them in his *Paris Journals* as being 'mounted in ormolu' and costing him 25 louis (with other china). He gave them a prominent position in the 'Gallery' of his villa at Strawberry Hill, near Twickenham, and, after the sale of its contents in 1842, the vases passed into Lord Morley's collection before being acquired by Baron Ferdinand. The restrained classical style of the *ormolu* mounts, especially of the pedestals, was remarkably avant-garde in 1765 and indicates that they had probably been commissioned in Paris only a short time before Horace Walpole made the purchase. Their design successfully complements the shape of the Urbino vases, adding a touch of distinction to them, and it seems regrettable that, although other spectacular Italian maiolica vases were undoubtedly mounted in *ormolu* by the French, this pair seem to be the only examples to have survived with a complete and fully recorded pedigree.

Among the small but choice selection of Italian maiolica of the Late Renaissance in the Bequest are two important 'pilgrim-bottles', both decorated with the so-called 'grotesque' style that had become very popular by the 1570s. Despite their apparent similarity, they are not a pair (as previously published) and were undoubtedly made for two different persons of high rank, the Duke of Ferrara and the Count of Lemos, on two quite separate occasions. One of the two bottles (Fig.20) was probably made in 1579 on the occasion of the marriage of Alfonso II d'Este, Duke of Ferrara, and Margarita Gonzaga, for it bears the same motto (ARDET AETERNUM) and device (a flaming pyre) as occur on the reverse of the medal struck in their honour at the time of their marriage. The bottle was evidently part of a large service, for a number of similarly decorated pieces survive, and, though there is no conclusive evidence, it seems likely that the service was made in Urbino, perhaps in the workshop of the Patanazzi family. The roundel on either side is painted with figures that may have been intended to represent two of the Four Seasons: Bacchus holding bunches of grapes (for Autumn) and an old man warming himself at a fire (for Winter); a companion bottle might, therefore, have been made with representations of Spring and Summer.

The other pilgrim-bottle (Fig.21) is painted on both sides with the coat of arms of the Count of Lemos. The heraldic charges of this complicated achievement must have taxed the skill of the maiolica-painter, who probably had little understanding of the subtleties of Spanish heraldry. Nevertheless, the arms are accurately copied, albeit without great finesse, and the painter has consistently distinguished between *gules* (red) and *or* (gold) by using a dark and a light shade of yellow respectively. Undoubtedly, the arms belong to a Count of Lemos, of the House of Castro-Portugal, one of the original grandeeships of Spain; the most likely is the sixth Count (1548–1601) since his arms, emblazoned in 1600 in the Register of the Confraternity of St Martha (State Archives, Naples), correspond with those on the bottle. Significantly, his arms include the red cross of the Order of Calatrava, which he entered in 1575, and as the maiolica-painter had carefully depicted (in the orange pigment used for red) the ends of the cross of the Order projecting from the escutcheon, this bottle cannot have been made for him before 1575, which was also the year of his embassy to Pope Gregory XIII. Although the bottle could have been made subsequently at any time before his death in Naples, where for two years (1599–1601) he held the post of viceroy, nevertheless, on stylistic grounds, the bottle would seem to have been made in Italy, probably at Urbino, about 1575 or very soon afterwards.

5. French Renaissance Painted Enamels

Whereas the Italian maiolica-painters had been the first in Europe to fire brilliant polychrome pictures on to simple earthenware and the Venetian glassmakers had been the pioneers in enamelled painting on glass, it was the craftsmen of Limoges, in the centre of France, who completely transformed the traditional craft of enamelling on copper. They gave this art a new dimension by developing a totally different technique: instead of engraving or gouging out channels in the copper to receive the enamel, as had been the practice since the twelfth century, they treated the surface of the copper like an artist's canvas. The outlines of the composition of the picture would first be delineated, often by scratching with a metal point through a layer of opaque enamel, still in its wet, unfired state, and then the rest of the picture would be filled in with coloured enamels applied in layers and fixed in a succession of firings, until finally the completed composition would be ready to be enhanced by touches of gilding, fired at a much lower temperature. As on maiolica, the fired colours have a uniquely vivid, almost luminous, tonality, which was often enhanced by the use of gold or silver foil beneath the translucent enamel so that the light, reflected back from the metal foil, intensified the brilliance of the colour of the enamel.

Like the Italian painters of maiolica, the French enamellers turned to woodcuts and engravings for inspiration and frequently copied the compositions in a quite slavish fashion. The Bequest contains one very interesting early example of this practice, the plaque of Aeneas leaving Carthage and bidding farewell to Dido (Colour Pl. VIII). It is one of a large set, of which seventy-four are known to have survived. All are closely copied from the woodcut illustrations of an edition of Virgil's *Opera*, edited by Sebastian Brant and first printed by Johann Grüninger in Strasburg in 1502, or, arguably, from one of the two subsequent editions printed at Lyons in 1517 and 1529, in which the same woodcuts were again used (Fig.22). There were 143 woodcuts in the first edition of Grüninger's Virgil, but no enamel plaque copied from any of the last three Books of the *Aeneid* is known. Because each plaque is a *unicum* and because it is rare in Limoges painted enamels to find no repetition or close variant of a subject, it may be assumed that the complete set must have been a very special commission, perhaps made to decorate the walls of a study or a cabinet of an eminent patron at the French court.

Neither the identity of the enameller nor the date at which the set was painted can be established with certainty. Of course, the Late Gothic style of the figures and of the composition of the narrative scenes is an accurate reflection of the work of the artist who made the woodcuts in 1502 and therefore does not help to date the plaque, but certain technical aspects of the enamelling indicate a date of manufacture after the first quarter of the sixteenth century. Each copper plaque in the set was first silvered and then the composition delineated in russet lines directly on to the metal. A tan-coloured translucent enamel is used for large areas, thereby permitting the metal to shine through. Many details are picked out in gold and most of the shading is executed in black, whilst foil is sparingly used for the dresses. Because the attribution of this set to the ageing Jean I Pénicaud, who is not recorded after 1543, seems unconvincing, it is probably better to retain the earlier formula and simply state that it was painted by the unknown 'Master of the Aeneid Series', probably about 1530–40.

The Limoges enamellers, who had at first tended to copy from German woodcuts and engravings, especially the works of Dürer, later turned their attention to contemporary Italian engravings. One of the most spectacular examples in the Bequest is the large composite panel of scenes from the *Aeneid* (Figs.23,24), in which ten separate plaques have been copied directly from an engraving by Marcantonio Raimondi entitled *Quos Ego* (a reference to the interrupted threat made by Neptune to the Winds, Book I, verse 135). The engraving (Fig.25) was probably designed to be used as a frontispiece to an Italian edition of Virgil, and the central composition of Neptune in

Fig. 22 'Aeneas leaving Carthage and bidding farewell to Dido'. This woodcut, the source for the Limoges painted enamel plaque (see Colour Pl. VIII), was first printed in Strasburg in 1502 in Sebastian Brant's edition of Virgil's *Opera*; it was reused in the French editions published at Lyons in 1517 and 1529.

his chariot stilling the winds is thought to derive from a lost painting by Raphael. Each of the ten plaques is stamped on the back with the punch-mark used in the Pénicaud workshop under Jean II Pénicaud and probably dates from about 1540–50. The extremely subtle nuances of the painting of the Neptune panel (in the centre) are undoubtedly indicative of the hand of the master himself, but the other nine polychrome panels are possibly the work of assistants.

For a short period during the middle of the sixteenth century, the grisaille technique (white painting on a dark ground) seems to have been preferred to the polychrome

Fig. 24 (*Left*) 'Neptune addressing the Winds' (*Aeneid*, Book I, verse 135). This central plaque exemplifies the quality of Jean II Pénicaud's work. Limoges, *c*.1540–50. H. 10¾ in (27.3 cm); W. 8 in (20.3 cm).

Fig. 23 (*Above*) The *Quos Ego* panel, composed of 10 enamelled plaques painted with scenes from the *Aeneid*. Each plaque is stamped (on the reverse under the counter-enamel) with the punch-mark of the Pénicaud workshop in Limoges. This punch-mark was much in use under Jean II Pénicaud, probably the eldest son of Nardon Pénicaud and perhaps the same man who in 1540 and again in 1548 was elected consul, together with Jean Poillevé, the goldsmith. The 5 plaques with inscriptions have no punch-marks and are modern additions; the four small plaques were re-assembled in the wrong order. H. 19¾ in (50.2 cm). W. 17 in (43.2 cm).

Fig. 25 (*Above right*) *Quos Ego*. The central scene is thought to be after a lost painting by Raphael. This engraving is the work of the celebrated Italian engraver, Marcantonio Raimondi (active in Rome, first quarter of 16th century).

and, in the hands of the great masters of this craft, the most sophisticated and subtle effects were achieved. One of the earliest examples is a casket preserved in the Bequest (Colour Pl. XIVB) which, because it still retains its original silver-gilt mounts, can be dated fairly precisely to around 1530–5. Although the silver mounts on this casket no longer bear any legible hallmarks and, consequently, neither the maker, the town nor the year of manufacture can be established with certainty, two mother-of-pearl caskets have recently been examined and found to have not only silver mounts so similar in design and workmanship that all three caskets must have been made in the same workshop, but also legible Paris hallmarks and the same maker's mark, a B. The mother-of-pearl casket preserved in the Treasury of the Cathedral of Mantua bears the hallmark of Paris and the date-letter for 1533–34, whilst the other mother-of-pearl casket, formerly in the Earl of Chesterfield's collection and now in a private collection, bears the Paris hallmarks for 1532–33. The maker's mark, which is stamped on both the mother-of-pearl caskets, has been tentatively identified as the mark of Jacques Barbe or a member of the Barbedor family of goldsmiths in Paris, and there can be little doubt that the same goldsmith made the casket in the Waddesdon Bequest, which, in place of the mother-of-pearl, has been set with painted enamel plaques in the very latest fashion.

This casket with its enamelled plaques probably dates, therefore, from the mid-1530s and, as such, is among the earliest-known examples of the use of the grisaille technique in the field of Renaissance painted enamels. The beautiful half-length figures painted in white with subtle flesh tints on a black ground represent eight of the twelve Sibyls, those women in the classical world who were reputed to possess the gift of prophecy. Beside each figure the name has been added in gold, though, in fact, each holds the

45

appropriate attribute – for example, the Libyan Sibyl carries the lighted torch. The enamel plaque on the lid bears the initials IP, which is one of several forms of signature used by the enigmatic 'Master KIP', who has been most unconvincingly identified with Jean Poillevé, a goldsmith of substance mentioned in various Limoges documents between 1537 and 1555. Another casket in the Bequest (Fig.26), with more skilfully painted miniatures in grisaille and explanatory inscriptions in French painted in gold, is composed of twelve small plaques depicting the story of Tobit, but none is signed. This gifted enameller may have been a member of the Pénicaud workshop and can perhaps be identified with an anonymous enameller who occasionally signed his works, M.P. Whatever may be his correct identity, this enameller's subtle delicacy of the gradations of tone shows a complete mastery of the technique of grisaille enamelling and this casket probably dates from the 1540s.

Painted enamels moved to the forefront of the decorative arts of the French

Fig. 26 Casket composed of 12 enamelled plaques, painted in grisaille with the story of Tobit; the figures are interestingly depicted wearing contemporary costume. Probably by the enameller known as the Master M.P. or a member of the Pénicaud family. Limoges, c.1540–50. H. 4⅜ in (11.1 cm).

Renaissance when the King's counsellor and ambassador, Jean de Langeac (Bishop of Limoges, 1533–41), introduced a young and talented enameller, Léonard Limosin, to the court at Fontainebleau, just at the moment when two great Italian Mannerist painters, Rosso (died 1540) and Primaticcio (working there 1532–70), were making a revolutionary contribution to the art of the Renaissance. Léonard Limosin absorbed the new style of the Fontainebleau School of painting and became its chief exponent in the field of enamel-painting. Working extensively for two French kings, François I (died 1547) and Henri II (died 1559), he saw his works used to decorate royal palaces and chapels, as well as the principal rooms of the great houses of the nobility. According to Pierre Guilbert in 1731, his enamel plaques had been set alongside the frescoes and stucco decorations in the ceiling and the panelling of the famous *Gallérie de François I* at the Palace of Fontainebleau; certainly, the two retables made for altars in the choir of the Sainte-Chapelle in Paris, which he finished in 1553 for Henri II, still survive (in the Musée du Louvre); similarly, the large enamel plaques of the twelve Apostles, which were commissioned by François I shortly before his death and which were later presented by Henri II to his mistress, Diane de Poitiers, for the chapel of her newly built château at Anet, can still be seen (in the Musée des Beaux-Arts, Chartres). The inventories show that many of his enamelled *objets d'art* were kept in the *Cabinet des Bagues* (Jewel Room) in the Palace of Fontainebleau and that the Queen Mother, Catherine de Medici, when she died in 1589, not only had chests full of enamelled objects but her *cabinet des emaux* was decorated with enamelled portraits set in the panelling of the room.

In the Waddesdon Bequest this artist, who was also an engraver and a painter, is represented by two fine portraits. The earlier (Colour Pl. IXA) is important because it is not only signed but is dated 1550, just two years after he had been made a '*valet de chambre du Roy*' by Henri II. The unknown man, whose adolescent face is so penetratingly portrayed, was probably a young nobleman at court, but, despite its quality, it may not have been painted from the life but merely copied with great sensitivity from a miniature or small oil-painting by one of the leading court artists, such as François Clouet or Corneille de Lyon. In the other Léonard Limosin portrait (Fig.27), the identity of the sitter is well attested and consequently this large and brilliantly enamelled portrait bust can be dated fairly accurately to the early 1570s. It represents the daughter of the duc de Guise, Catherine of Lorraine, who in 1570, at the age of eighteen, married Louis de Bourbon, duc de Montpensier, whose portrait was also painted in enamel by Léonard Limosin. As Léonard Limosin died between 1575 and 1577, this plaque offers valuable evidence of his style and the high standards he maintained towards the end of his distinguished career. The young face is subtly modelled by a technique of minute stippling, mainly in shades of red, but, like many court portraits in the Mannerist style, it has a frozen mask-like quality that hides the tempestuous nature of this remarkable woman, whose political intrigues rocked the throne of France. In one respect this panel is unusual, for the signature appears on a white puff on the left shoulder of her dress and, instead of being written, the letters are pricked out in dots.

In Limoges, the many gifted contemporaries of Léonard Limosin continued throughout the sixteenth century to transmit through the media of painted enamels the elegant style of French Mannerism. A seemingly endless repertoire of Mannerist scenes and strap-work designs, in part created by Italian artists and the Fontainebleau School

Fig. 27 Catherine of Lorraine depicted shortly after her marriage at the age of 18 to Louis de Bourbon, duc de Montpensier, in 1570.
This painted enamel portrait is a late work of Léonard Limosin (*c.* 1505–75/7), who as early as 1536 had enamelled a portrait of
François i's Queen, Eleanor of Austria. H. 12 in (30.5 cm).

but also greatly enriched by French engravers, like Androuet du Cerceau and Étienne Delaune, provided the Limoges workshops with their sources of inspiration.

A striking example dating from the end of the sixteenth century is the magnificent large oval dish of Apollo on Mount Helicon, accompanied by the winged horse Pegasus and surrounded by the nine Muses (Colour Pl. IXB). In the foreground of the composition is the prominent signature, SVSANNE COVRT; however, this very competent Limoges enameller was not in the least responsible for the design, which is copied from an engraving by Giorgio Ghisi of Mantua, who in turn had based it on a drawing by Luca Penni, who had been inspired by Raphael's great fresco, *Parnassus* (or Marcantonio Raimondi's engraved version of it), in the *Stanza della Segnatura* in the Vatican Palace. The engraver, Giorgio Ghisi, was a gifted artist, whose brilliant skills in an allied field, the art of damascening, can be studied on the famous shield of 1554, which is preserved in the Bequest (Colour Pl. XIIB). Subsequently, Ghisi's engraving of Apollo and the Muses was re-engraved in France by Gaspar ab Avibus (published 1563) and by Étienne Delaune; furthermore, several other enamellers at Limoges, including Jean de Court, the most distinguished member of the Court family, produced their own slightly varied adaptations.

The popularity of the subject may have been due to its relevance to the development of the Renaissance garden, with its emphasis on rocks, water, grottoes and music. According to the ancient Greek writers, Mount Helicon had begun to ascend towards heaven at the sound of the music being played by Apollo and the Muses, but Pegasus stopped its ascent by stamping on the ground; however, the waters of the sacred stream Hippocrene immediately gushed forth at every spot where the hooves of Pegasus had struck. By the second half of the sixteenth century, the designers of the great Mannerist gardens added a new ingredient to their grottoes and fountains, the element of surprise: fine jets of water would spring without warning from the floors or the walls of the grottoes, soaking the distinguished visitor, even the Emperor Charles V himself. In France these 'wetting sports' (as an English traveller aptly called them) were popular with that talented court designer and potter, Bernard Palissy, who was famous for his grottoes and the realism of his ceramic effects. He devised a garden statue that held a vase of water in one hand and a text in the other, ready to empty the water on to the head of the visitor whose curiosity led him to get close enough to read the words of the text. In 1563 Palissy wrote in *Recepte véritable* that hidden mechanical music should issue forth in certain parts of the garden, as if he wished to re-create the Mount Helicon of antiquity, which was probably as popular a subject with his readers as with the patrons of the enamellers of Limoges. Indeed, the very conception of the gardens and the fountains at the palace of Fontainebleau seems to have been a recreation of Parnassus itself.

Because enamelling in Limoges was often a family skill, many of the workshops continued through several generations – the Pénicaud, the Limosin, the Reymond, the Nouailher, the Courteys and the Laudin dynasties, for example. Consequently, it is not always easy to distinguish with certainty the *œuvre* of one member of the family from another, especially when, as often happens, they bear the same Christian name. Many of the best productions of these great families are represented in the Waddesdon Bequest, but their works, although most skilfully executed, demonstrate again and again the reliance they placed on engravings as a source of inspiration.

6. Renaissance Jewellery

The art of enamelling was an essential part of the jeweller's skills throughout the Renaissance, for gold jewellery, although often profusely set with gems and precious stones, was frequently fashioned into some piece of miniature sculpture, each part being coloured in enamel, and the remaining surfaces of the gold (including the backs of the jewels) were often enriched with intricate designs executed in coloured enamels. This richly polychrome effect is a striking characteristic of Renaissance jewellery matched only by the whimsical ingenuity of its three-dimensional sculptural forms. In neither respect is it reminiscent of jewellery of classical antiquity; indeed, apart from the art of cameo-carving and gem-engraving, there was no rebirth of Greek or Roman jewellery during the Renaissance. Instead, the Renaissance goldsmith developed a new vocabulary of ornamental designs and motifs (putti, dolphins, satyrs, grotesques, scroll-work, strap-work, etc.) that led to the creation of jewellery entirely different from the Gothic, although continuing to favour figural subjects.

The wearing of jewellery in Early Renaissance Italy during the fifteenth century was far more restrained than in the following century and seems connected with the discovery of human beauty and the nude, which spread from Florence through the courts of Ferrara, Mantua and Urbino to Venice and Rome – and eventually to the rest of Europe. As a result, women's hair was no longer hidden beneath coifs, wimples and elaborate head-dresses but, entwined with strings of pearls and aigrettes of precious stones, it was allowed to flow freely in tresses or to be gathered up to reveal the full beauty of the neck. The neck-line of the dress steadily fell further and further during the second half of the fifteenth century, displaying more and more of the neck and shoulders, until the true *décolletage* of the sixteenth century was reached. In consequence, the brooch was almost completely replaced by the pendant jewel, to emphasise the beauty of the breast, and the necklace, often set with pearls, to set off the slender column of the neck. Ear-rings could once more be worn, and again the pendant pearl was a strong favourite. Although finger-rings continued to be worn, the Late Gothic fashion of wearing several rings on each finger (and even on the thumb) ceased; it became *de rigueur* to wear no more than two or three. For men, the wearing of jewellery was even more restrained, mainly finger-rings and hat medallions.

Few jewels of the Early Renaissance have survived; in the Bequest, one of the finest hat medallions of the first half of the sixteenth century depicts the Conversion of St Paul (Colour Pl. xA). Within this tiny roundel, the goldsmith has created an animated crowded scene of people and horses, of buildings and precious stones. The goldsmith, first working from the back (the repoussé technique) to create in high relief the main elements of the composition, then working on the front (the chasing technique) to create the minute details of modelling, has applied coloured translucent and opaque enamels, which were skilfully fired on at different temperatures, and finally, the diamonds and rubies have been set into the scene, for example, on the pilasters of the building or the shields of St Paul's companions. Benvenuto Cellini (1500-71), in his technical *Treatises*, gives a detailed account of the painstaking skills by which he tried to outshine his great rival, Caradosso (died 1527), in the creation of these gold enamelled hat medallions. Though no surviving example can be attributed either to Cellini or to Caradosso, this hat jewel of the Conversion of St Paul is made in the same manner and is a veritable *tour de force* of miniature sculpture in the Renaissance style.

By the second half of the sixteenth century the harmonious relationship between body, clothes and jewelled adornment had given way to a formal, artificially contrived magnificence of stiff heavy brocades and velvets, often of sombre black, purple and deep violets, encrusted with a profusion of pearls, gem-stones and gold enamelled jewels of bizarre design and fantastic inventiveness. The body was once more encased beneath a glittering façade until only the head and hands remained visible – and even these were severely constricted by the starched ruffs and the elaborate high lace collars and cuffs, from which pendant jewels were hung. Men were no less bedecked in jewellery than women; in England, for example, James I (reigned 1603–25) was portrayed in as sumptuously a gem-studded attire as Queen Elizabeth I before him. This new style was dictated by the powerful court of Spain, politically dominant in Europe and immensely rich through its possessions in the New World. Known as the 'Spanish Style', it prevailed throughout the courts of Europe from about 1550 to 1630, and it is the jewellery from this era that has mostly survived and has been generally labelled 'Renaissance Jewellery'.

The Waddesdon Bequest contains many splendid examples, from finger-rings to lockets, but is especially rich in those heavy sculptural pendants that were so distinctive a feature of the jewellery of this period, particularly in Germany where Erasmus Hornick was publishing his engraved designs for this type of jewellery in the 1560s. A massive 'architectural' jewel with a free-standing figure group of Charity and three

Fig. 28 Reverse of the 'Charity' gold enamelled pendant (see Colour Pl. x); the bold architectural design in low relief, enamelled in white, blue and red, complements the architectural treatment of the front of the weighty jewel. H. 3¾ in (9.4 cm).

children in the centre (Colour Pl. xA, Fig.28) bears a general similarity to several of Hornick's designs published in Nuremberg in 1565, but it may not have been made by Hornick himself, for although he was trained as a goldsmith in his native Antwerp, there is no piece of jewellery or plate that can be identified as his work with certainty. This is most unfortunate because he was clearly a very considerable success – and not just as a disseminator of designs for jewellery and plate. At first he settled in Augsburg, a great centre for goldsmiths, and in 1555 married the daughter of a patrician family there. After spending six or seven years in Nuremberg, he returned to Augsburg where he was granted citizenship; his death occurred in 1585, the year after he had joined the court of the Emperor Rudolf II in Prague and, once again, there is no evidence that he actually made a piece for the Emperor. The maker of this magnificent pendant, whoever he was, must rank as one of the leading craftsmen in Europe at this time (about 1560–70), combining the skilful setting of diamonds, rubies and emeralds with the brilliant use of enamel, not only for the figures of the Virtues, the putti and the lions but also for every detail of the scrolls, the masks and the bunches of fruit – even the back, where a most unusual architectural design is carried out in enamel on the gold.

This same artist, Erasmus Hornick, published two engraved designs for toothpicks (Fig.29) in Nuremberg in 1562, but the example in the Bequest was probably made later in the sixteenth century and exemplifies the more sophisticated Mannerist approach (Colour Pl. xA). Using a natural phenomenon – a large, irregularly shaped 'baroque' pearl – as a starting-point, the goldsmith has interpreted its irregular form and created around it in enamelled gold a fabulous mermaid-like creature. There is no evidence that Hornick intended a 'baroque' pearl to be used for the torso, especially as he made almost identical designs for spoon and fork handles. However, during the Late Renaissance this type of jewel became very fashionable, and the Bequest contains several fine examples, one of which is a fantastic sea-dragon (Colour Pl. xB, Fig.30).

In this jewel, two large 'baroque' pearls have been ingeniously used to create the body and the tail of this sea-monster, and several small pearls are cunningly used to disguise the join where the tail begins. Whilst the engraved designs of Erasmus Hornick in 1562 and of Hans Collaert of Antwerp in 1581 include large pendants in the form of dragons and sea-horses, they do not seem to incorporate the 'baroque' pearl – unlike the drawing of a similar pendant by the Spanish apprentice Pere Juan Bastons in 1593 (preserved in Barcelona). Indeed, a Spanish origin for this sea-dragon pendant seems likely, for the most comparable piece to have survived – and it certainly comes from the same workshop – is preserved in the Cathedral Treasury of Santo Domingo (Dominican Republic). A Spanish origin for the Waddesdon toothpick also seems to be most probable, but the dangerous pursuit of 'nationality attributions' in this international field of Renaissance court jewellery is to be avoided unless the evidence is overwhelmingly clear. Not only did the goldsmiths and jewellers move from court to court but the engraved designs were quickly circulated and the patrons were always anxious to be à la mode. Little wonder, therefore, that this toothpick in the Waddesdon Bequest has recently been illustrated twice in different chapters of the same book, once as a jewel originating in Southern Germany and once as coming from Spain; at least there is no disagreement about its probable date of origin in the late sixteenth century.

The huge pendants were intended to be worn over the rich brocades, perhaps pinned high up on the stiff sleeves so that they were free to swing freely, catching the light as they moved. Some of the massive pendants in the Bequest are set with large

Fig. 29 (*Left*) Two designs for toothpicks engraved by Erasmus Hornick and published in Nuremberg in 1562.

Fig. 30 (*Above*) Reverse of the sea-dragon pendant jewel (see Colour Pl. XB); the enamelled gold body provides the essential support and strong setting for the large 'baroque' pearl forming the body of the sea-dragon on the front. W. 3⅞ in (9.8 cm).

Fig. 31 (*Above right*) Gold enamelled pendant jewel: a monstrous fish ridden by a primitive warrior, perhaps an Aztec Indian, set with emeralds, amethysts and garnets. Spanish, end of 16th century. L. 3⅞ in (9.8 cm).

cabochon emeralds, brought to Spain no doubt from the rich deposits in the New World; a finer example than the hippocamp pendant (Colour Pl. XB) would be hard to find. The sense of writhing movement and curving three-dimensional form makes this pendant superficially akin to the engraved design of Erasmus Hornick in 1562, but the scale and relationship of the rider to the hippocamp is very different from that of the riders in Hornick's designs. The rider on this jewel is a curious female, bare-breasted and long-haired; she wears only a skirt and sits side-saddle on the sea-horse. In no sense does she conform to the Northern European Mannerist creatures that men like Hornick, Collaert or Assuerus van Londerseel in Antwerp were publishing in their engravings. This female figure, with her strange head-dress (perhaps of feathers), can be likened to an American Indian, and the jewel seen as an indirect consequence of Spain's exploration of the New World. Certainly, the hippocamp's forelegs terminate in the same distinctive small fin-like scroll that is such a prominent feature of the 1777 *Inventario* drawing of a Triton pendant jewel (fol. 45v.) preserved in the Archivo del Real Monasterio, Guadalupe.

Perhaps the strangest of these sea-creatures is the monstrous fish ridden by a warrior (Fig. 31), which closely resembles two jewels that are depicted in the watercolour illustrations (fols. 1 and 43) of the *Inventario* of 1777. Two other drawings of similar monstrous fish pendants, both dated 1586, are preserved among the examinees' drawings of the goldsmiths' guild in Barcelona. As the great maritime power exploring the New World, Spain would have been filled with stories of the horrors of man-eating sharks and killer-whales, and it is understandable that these terrifying creatures entered the repertoire of the Spanish goldsmiths of the Late Renaissance.

Fig. 32 (*Right*) The Lyte Jewel, set with 29 diamonds, its pierced openwork cover of enamelled gold forming the monogram, IR (IACOBUS REX). Presented by King James I to Thomas Lyte in 1610 with his likeness painted by Nicholas Hilliard (see Colour Pl. XIA). H. 2½ in (6.4 cm).

Fig. 33 (*Far right*) Reverse of the Lyte Jewel, with its elegant gold and enamelled design derived from a French engraving, perhaps by Daniel Mignot.

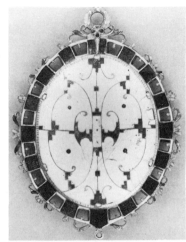

Fig. 34 (*Left*) Thomas Lyte, of Lyte's Carey, Somerset, aged 43, wearing the Jewel on a silk ribbon; a panel portrait dated 14 April 1611. (Preserved in the Somerset County Museum, Taunton).

Fig. 35 (*Above*) Detail of the portrait (Fig. 34) showing the Lyte Jewel complete with its original diamond-set drop, of unique trilobed form. Both the portrait and the Jewel remained at Lyte's Carey until 1747, and subsequently the drop became separated from the Jewel (before 1882).

During the second half of the sixteenth century, the jewelled locket became an increasingly important item of jewellery, especially for men, for it became fashionable to keep within it a miniature portrait of the lady who was the object of the wearer's affections. Men usually wore these lockets on a ribbon or silk scarf around the neck, so that the locket would hang down on the chest and could be easily opened and gazed upon. These lockets were usually made of gold, elaborately enamelled and often studded with gems and set with cameos. Of the three in the Waddesdon Bequest, the finest is unquestionably the famous Lyte Jewel (Colour Pl. XIA), which was designed to contain a miniature of King James I, who presented this jewel to Thomas Lyte in 1610.

This historic locket of enamelled gold is set with twenty-five square table-cut diamonds and four faceted-cut diamonds. The cover (Fig.32) has a pierced open-work design mainly composed of the monogram IR (in Latin, IACOBUS REX) for King James VI of Scotland and I of England, who succeeded Queen Elizabeth in 1603. The cover is hinged and lifts up to reveal the King's likeness painted by Nicholas Hilliard (1547–1619). Appointed painter, limner and engraver to Queen Elizabeth I and, subsequently, to James I, Nicholas Hilliard was the first English-born artist to gain this recognition at court. His talents as a miniaturist and portraitist deservedly gained for him, both at home and abroad, a fame that few English artists have enjoyed. He was also a goldsmith and may well have designed this jewel to be the perfect setting for his miniature of the King. At that time, such jewels were regarded as a single unit – the limned likeness and its locket were one; for this reason, the limner's colours retained the intensity of enamel or precious stones, as Hilliard in his treatise on the *Art of Limning* explains in unambiguous detail. Certainly, the brilliant enamelled decoration on the inside of the cover complements in a subtle way the colours of the miniature itself. In contrast, the enamelled back of the locket is principally white with a highly sophisticated design carried out in thin gold lines and a little ruby-coloured enamel. French engravers, such as Daniel Mignot in 1590, began to create these curiously mannered versions of the mid-sixteenth-century mauresque patterns, but very few jewels have survived to illustrate their application by goldsmiths – and none is more successful than the back of this English royal jewel (Fig.33).

Thomas Lyte received this handsome present as a reward for drawing up a pedigree of the King, in which his ancestry was traced back without a break to the mythical founder of the British nation, Brut, the Trojan. When this Somerset gentleman had his portrait painted in the following year, 1611, he was shown proudly wearing this jewel on a red silk ribbon (Fig.34), and it is interesting to note that, instead of the modern pendant pearl, the locket originally had a trilobed drop set with diamonds hanging from the tiny loop at the base, and in a subtle way the design of this jewel then seems perfectly complete (Fig.35).

Although many of the Continental engraved designs for such miniature cases about 1610 offered the goldsmith a bewildering choice of elegant, thinly drawn patterns *en silhouette*, there remained, especially in England, a taste for the bolder and more geometric strap-work ornament. A large and exceptionally fine English gold enamelled miniature case in the Waddesdon Bequest (Colour Pl. XIA) is a rare example of this style, recalling the designs of Corvinianus Saur, the South German goldsmith who became court goldsmith to King Christian IV of Denmark (reigned 1588–1648) and who published designs for engraved ornament between 1591 and 1597. Close connections existed at this time between Denmark and England; not only was Christian IV's sister Anne married to James I of England, but the Danish king paid a state visit to the English court in 1606. The strong radiating design in white enamel, with delicate details in gold, gives the impression of being superimposed on a subdued background composed of subtly transformed moresque designs in gold on a black enamel ground. When used on its own, this use of gold patterns silhouetted against a black enamel ground often achieved a dignified, sombre, even dramatic, effect – perhaps no more so than on the crown, orb and sceptre of Queen Kristina of Sweden (1573–1625), with which she was buried in the cathedral of Strängnäs in 1626 and which since 1980 have been in the *Livrustkammaren* in the Royal Palace, Stockholm.

The second gem-studded locket complete with its original miniature preserved in the Bequest (Colour Pl. XIA-C) was also made in England but a quarter of a century later than the Lyte Jewel. It, too, is a magnificent example of enamelled goldsmiths' work in harmony with the art of gem-setting, but it also demonstrates most vividly how taste and style had changed within those twenty-five years. Unlike the Lyte Jewel, this locket was acquired by Baron Ferdinand direct from the lineal descendants of the first owner, Sir Bevil Grenville (1595–1643), the Cornish Royalist general. His widow's will, dated 19 April 1647, mentions 'two jewels or pictures' which are bequeathed to her two daughters, Lady Prideaux and Mrs Robert Fortescue. Lady Prideaux's jewel appears to have remained at Hall in North Devon until its departure to Waddesdon Manor late in the nineteenth century. It contains a miniature portrait of a man in armour with a falling lace collar, long hair, a moustache and beard; it is signed D.D.G. (David Des Granges). This artist was born a Huguenot, the son of Samson Des Granges of Guernsey. Baptised in London on either 24 May 1611 or 20 January 1613, David Des Granges was later to become a friend of Inigo Jones, that great English Renaissance *uomo universale*. In 1628, he produced his engraving after Raphael's painting of *St George and the Dragon*, which had been brought to England in 1506 as a gift to King Henry VII from the Duke of Urbino, on whom the Order of the Garter had been conferred. David Des Granges, employed by both Charles I and Charles II, went with the King to Scotland in 1651 and was there appointed His Majesty's limner.

Des Granges's earliest dated miniature known to have survived is signed 'D.D.G.' and bears the date 1639; it is preserved in Windsor Castle and is said to represent Catherine Manners, Duchess of Buckingham. It would seem that the portrait of Sir Bevil Grenville in the Waddesdon locket must also date from this early period. Although the quality of this miniature cannot compare with the large portrait of Sir Bevil painted in 1636, which has survived in the Cornish branch of the family and which is attributed to Van Dyke, the face does bear a close resemblance. However, there are so many differences that it seems most unlikely that the miniature was copied from the large portrait. Indeed, the miniature suggests that the sitter is older than in the 1636 picture and may, therefore, have been commissioned about 1640.

The locket itself is a brilliantly polychrome carpet of enamelling on both front and back, incorporating pansies, marguerites and leaves; the hinged front is enriched with a large sapphire in the centre, surrounded by rubies, opals and diamonds and two emeralds. The total effect is as unrestrained and colourful as a herbaceous border in a summer garden. No trace of the disciplined Mannerist elegance of the Lyte Jewel remains nor is there any tonal relationship between the miniature and its gold setting, such as was sought by Hilliard. An exquisite rarity, this locket with its sound documentary significance, is vital evidence of English court taste on the eve of the Civil War.

7. Renaissance Metalwork

In the Renaissance, a distinction seems to have existed between those goldsmiths who made large-scale gold and silver plate and those who produced the small-scale work, like jewellery. Benvenuto Cellini, the only practising goldsmith of the Renaissance to write a technical account of the craft, makes the distinction very firmly in his *Treatise on Goldsmithing*; he has a separate chapter on 'How to fashion vessels of gold and silver, likewise figures and vases, and all that pertains to that branch of the craft called "grosseria"' and he has another chapter on 'minuterie' which he defines as 'all that class of work done with a punch, such as rings and pendants and bracelets'. Cellini goes on to include under that second heading a discussion of the technical problems of making hat medallions and of his famous salt-cellar for François I (now in the Kunsthistorisches Museum, Vienna). Although Cellini and one or two other eminent goldsmiths, such as his counterpart in Germany, Wenzel Jamnitzer, may have worked equally in both branches, they seem to have been the exceptions, for normally a goldsmith appears to have been trained in one or other of the two skills.

In the Bequest, there are a number of small-scale pieces of goldsmiths' work other than jewellery that must have been made by those trained in the art of 'minuterie' – items like the beautifully enamelled gold handles of the Dutch wedding knives and forks and the gold enamelled mounts on the engraved rock-crystals and the polished hard-stone vessels. Perhaps the most unusual and puzzling is the famous carved agate vase of Late Roman style with a gold enamelled foot, neck and cover published by some authorities as the work of Cellini himself (Fig.36). There is no documentary evidence to support this attribution, and all the complexities of the evidence will be analysed and discussed in full in the forthcoming Catalogue. In the interim, this account of the Bequest provides a valuable opportunity to publish two important new discoveries. Both are coloured drawings of the vase; neither is very competently executed and, though almost certainly of seventeenth-century origin, neither could have been the work of an artist of any standing.

The drawing entitled *Agathe Oriental* (Fig.37) has been preserved in the collections of the Dukes of Devonshire at Chatsworth, apparently from the mid-eighteenth century, if not before. Significantly, the vase itself was acquired from the Duke of Devonshire by Baron Ferdinand just before he died in 1898, perhaps as a result of seeing it at the Exhibition of Enamels at the Burlington Fine Arts Club in 1897, to which the Duke had lent it. Curiously, the Chatsworth drawing was neither exhibited with the vase nor sold to Baron Ferdinand. Many of the minor differences between the vase and the drawing, such as the shape of the handles, the satyr-heads below, the profile of the vase and the disposition of the vine-leaves and stems, might be dismissed as the result of incompetence on the part of an inferior artist, but the difference between the design on the vertical face of the foot is more difficult to explain. The reclining Bacchus in white enamel within a sunken oval panel and the rectangular fret on either side correspond closely, but the tiny vases in red enamel are two-handled amphorae whereas on the drawing these vases have no handles. In itself, this deviation might not seem so significant, but at each corner the goldsmith has included a vase, which is consequently bent in half at 90 degrees, leaving only half the vase on the front of the foot. No such eccentricity of design occurs in the drawing, where the corners are left empty (Fig.38).

The second drawing (Fig.37), which was purchased in London in 1885 by the Victoria and Albert Museum, has no earlier history, since it was part of a large collection of miscellaneous drawings bought from a dealer. However, it shows the vase from the same side and repeats most faithfully all these differences, although in some other respects this drawing does not slavishly reproduce all the details of the Chatsworth

Fig.36 Carved agate vase of Roman style, with gold enamelled mounts and cover, formerly attributed to Cellini. H. 8⅛ in (20.6 cm).

Fig. 37 Two coloured drawings:
(i) (*right*) with an inscription
Agathe Orientale; preserved in the
collections of the Duke of
Devonshire since the mid-18th
century, if not before; (ii) (*left*)
without any inscription or
history; purchased by the V & A
Museum in 1885 (unrecognised
in *Catalogue of Italian Drawings at
the V & A Museum*, Vol. 1 (1979),
no. 495). $8\frac{1}{2} \times 4\frac{3}{4}$ in
$(21.6 \times 12.1\,\text{cm})$.

Fig. 38 A detail from the
Chatsworth drawing compared
with the base of the
carved agate vase.

drawing. In other words, the London drawing does not seem to be a copy of the Chatsworth drawing and, though less competent, it nevertheless records the foot as being ornamented with handleless vases and plain empty corner spaces – not as it appears today. Similarly, the vase itself has a half-opened leaf carved in relief at the top on the right-hand vine stem (just below the neck), but neither drawing records this detail. As there is no ambiguity on either drawing in this area, unlike the neck and cover where both drawings are less than clear, it poses the serious question of how much reliance can be placed on these two drawings. Since the two drawings appear to have been executed quite independently of each other, the repetition of certain details in both drawings and the absence of these details on the object itself can only lead one to strike a note of caution pending the conclusion of the present investigation.

Regrettably, the Devonshire family papers have not yet provided any documentation for the vase earlier than 1892, and consequently its earlier history is still shrouded in uncertainty, along with the other four vases of hard-stone, also mounted in enamelled gold, which the Duke exhibited in 1897 and which Baron Ferdinand acquired shortly before his death in 1898.

Extremely talented work was being carried out in gold and silver by damascening on iron, especially on pieces of armour. The Bequest contains eight very fine examples of this skill, but for sheer virtuosity the famous shield by Giorgio Ghisi of Mantua (Colour Pl. XIIB) is probably unsurpassed. Never intended for use in battle, this parade shield is one of the masterpieces of Italian Mannerism in metalwork. Furthermore, it is a rare document being fully signed and dated: GEORGIUS DE GHISYS MNTVANZ FA M.D.LIIII. Born at Mantua in 1520, Giorgio Ghisi was well known as an engraver of prints and a contemporary, Giovanni Battista Bertano, called him 'a man truly at this day rare in the world of copper plates and in damascening work of the most diverse kinds'. Indeed, one of the French painted enamel dishes (Colour Pl. IXB) is copied from an engraving by Giorgio Ghisi. When he finished this shield in 1554, he proudly signed his masterpiece; a sword-hilt in the Budapest Museum seems to be the only other signed piece by this master to have survived. The elaborate scheme of the decoration, partly executed in bold relief and partly in extremely low relief, is dominated by the central roundel with its battle scene and the four surrounding panels containing the large emblematic figures of Glory, Fame, Strength and Prudence. Quickly the eye is led away by the linking pattern of strap-work, hung with festoons of fruit and ribbons, and soon discovers within it curious satyrs, strange bird-like creatures and leering masks, until finally the eye perceives the microscopic scenes contained within the frames of the five principal roundels; some are serious, like those of the Trojan Wars, others are mythological, and some are purely fanciful and, even, grotesque (Fig.39).

The new vocabulary of Italian Mannerist ornamental design, so richly represented in the Ghisi shield, can be seen on another splendid example of Italian metalwork in the Bequest – the beautiful bronze door-knocker from the Palazzo Martinengo-dobblo, in Brescia, near Milan (Fig.40). Although the coat of arms in the centre has been partially obliterated, it is possible to be certain about the origin of this bronze because the companion door-knocker, similarly defaced, was purchased in 1853 direct from one valve of the doors of the Palazzo by J. C. Robinson, who had been appointed 'art referee' to the newly created South Kensington Museum, now the Victoria and Albert Museum. In the 1876 *Catalogue of Bronzes at the South Kensington Museum*, Fortnum records that he had seen the companion knocker still hanging on the door of

Fig. 39 Prudence, framed by minute scenes from ancient mythology; a detail from the gold damascened shield of parade signed by Giorgio Ghisi of Mantua and dated 1554 (see Colour Pl. XIIB). H. 8½ in (21.6cm).

the Palazzo in Brescia in 1861, adding that it was one of the few knockers still remaining in the place for which it had been designed; it is not known when it entered Baron Ferdinand's collection. Its sophisticated flowing design combines many of the ingredients of Mannerist ornament – the tension of the imprisoned satyrs, the fluid forms of the dolphins and the serpents, and the vividly contrasting expressions on the faces of the two masks. Although the authorship of this bronze is uncertain, it can be dated to about the middle of the sixteenth century.

It is interesting to see in the Bequest how the goldsmiths of Northern Europe, particularly the makers of large silver plate, or 'grosseria', to use Cellini's term, absorbed this new language of ornament and gave it a slightly different and, perhaps, a less well-disciplined interpretation of their own. The silver plate in the Bequest is

Fig. 40 Bronze door-knocker, with the initials GC separated by a defaced shield of arms; from the Palazzo Martinengo-dobblo in Brescia, near Milan, middle of 16th century. H. 14 in (35.6 cm).

principally the work of German goldsmiths at the two great centres of Augsburg and Nuremberg, but there are a few important exceptions.

The historic Aspremont-Lynden ewer and basin (Figs.41–3) are early – and very rare – expressions of the new style from that great centre of Northern Mannerism, Antwerp. Made of silver gilt, the ewer bears the mark for 1544–5 and the basin for 1546–7. Although the egg-shaped body and general form of the ewer are based on Renaissance and classical originals, the design of the handle, the spout and the surface ornament is an extreme manifestation of Mannerist taste, as created by Italian artists and engravers. Even the pattern books rarely suggest a more complicated handle than the goldsmith has given this ewer, where one grotesque element evolves and subtly dissolves into another until, at the base, it divides into two tails which coil round and ensnare the arms of a satyr. The whole surface is embossed and chased with strap-work, entwined with snakes, and with curious monsters, Tritons, flower sprays and bunches of fruit – all the elements of Northern Mannerist ornament, in fact – but the final result lacks the purity and the discipline of the Italian sources.

The Aspremont-Lynden ewer and basin are first described in a document, in the Lynden family archives, dated 13 June 1610; thereafter, the records show that they remained together in the same family until shortly after 1880, when they had been seen at the National Exhibition in Brussels on loan from the Comtesse d'Aspremont-Lynden. The founder of this branch of the family, Robert de Lynden, seigneur de Froidcourt, vicomte de Dormael and Governor of Franchimont, died in 1610, but there is no indication of how or when he acquired this magnificent ewer and basin, which had been made more than fifty years earlier. Because the ewer and the basin are each stamped with a different maker's mark (neither is yet identified) and because the scenes on the basin depict the Plagues of Egypt and the Destruction of Pharoah's army, whereas the ewer is decorated with the figures of Neptune and Amphitrite, it has been suggested that these two pieces of silver may not have originally been made for each other, although they are remarkably well matched in other respects. Certainly, they exemplify the type of plate that was being commissioned by the wealthy patrons of rank throughout Northern Europe in the mid-sixteenth century.

Metalwork became an important art-form during the sixteenth century, for the ruler of every petty court in Europe aspired to the role of a Renaissance prince – a collector-prince, a patron of art and learning, surrounding himself with an ever-increasing display of opulent and extravagant works of art. Even in Northern Europe, to hunt and feast was not enough; instead, each prince began to build great galleries and libraries, and the jewel-house, which formerly housed the royal jewels and regalia, now developed into a treasure-house, filled with gold-mounted, gem-studded *objets d'art* and magnificent arrays of silver and gold plate, which would be set up on display whenever the ruler dined in state attended by his court or gave banquets in honour of visiting potentates. This precious plate was not intended for use – merely to be seen and envied as it stood amassed in tiers upon some large, open, cloth-covered 'sideboard' near the 'high table', at which the ruler and his honoured guests sat. Every piece of plate, therefore, had to excite wonder and admiration for the complexity of its design and the technical brilliance of its execution.

A second Antwerp silver ewer and basin in the Bequest (Figs.44–6) demonstrate the purely ostentatious nature of this kind of plate. Not only is the ewer elaborately embossed with strap-work enclosing Tritons but the main band around the body of the

Fig. 41 Silver-gilt ewer, embossed and chased; in centre of each side, a roundel with Neptune and Amphitrite, respectively. From the collection of the Counts of Aspremont-Lynden, first recorded in the family (together with the basin, Fig. 43) in 1610. Antwerp, 1544–5; maker's mark a pair of compasses. H. $13\frac{1}{2}$ in (34.3 cm).

Fig. 42 (*Left*) Detail of the Aspremont-Lynden ewer, with the Renaissance caryatid supporting the spout and fully developed Mannerist surface ornamentation, both reminiscent of the engraved designs by Cornelius Floris, based on Enea Vico, and published in Antwerp in 1548.

Fig. 43 (*Above*) Silver-gilt basin accompanying the ewer (Fig. 41), embossed and chased; scenes of the Plagues of Egypt and Pharaoh's army in the Red Sea. Central boss engraved with the arms of Robert de Lynden (1535–1610), seigneur de Froidcourt and vicomte de Dormael. Antwerp, 1546–7; maker's mark for Joris Weyer(?). Diam. 18½ in (4.7 cm).

Fig. 44 Silver ewer
accompanying the basin
(Fig. 45), embossed and chased;
Rape of Helen (after Raphael)
signed and dated by the chaser:
HR (in monogram), 1559.
Maker's mark, PS (in
monogram); no town mark.
Made in Antwerp, c.1558–9.

Fig. 45 Silver basin *en suite* with ewer (Fig. 44), embossed and chased with Judgement of Paris and (on the outer border) the Triumph of Neptune (after French engraving designed by du Cerceau) signed and dated by the chaser: HR (in monogram), 1558. Maker's mark, PS (in monogram); no town mark. Made in Antwerp, 1558. L. 19 in (48.3 cm).

Fig. 46 Detail of silver basin (Fig. 45) showing the chaser's signature and date on the embossed Triumph of Neptune outer border.

ewer has a well-composed figural scene in low relief depicting the Rape of Helen, derived from an Italian source. The form of the handle, with its satyr-like figure, is strikingly similar to some of the designs published in 1548 by Cornelis Floris, the Antwerp-born sculptor and architect, who in turn was copying extensively from the engraved designs published in Italy by Enea Vico in 1543. The finely embossed inner and outer borders on the oval basin are based on French Mannerist designs by Jacques Androuet du Cerceau, whose engravings helped to disseminate the stylistic innovations of the court school at Fontainebleau during the middle of the sixteenth century. A highly exceptional feature on both the ewer and the basin is that, in addition to the unknown maker's stamp, PS (in monogram), the embossed scenes are signed with the initials HR and the date 1558 (on the basin) and HR and 1559 (on the ewer). This second set of initials would seem to be those of the specialist master who carried out the embossing and chasing of the scenes in relief, which the goldsmith who made the ewer and basin evidently did not attempt to do himself. If this interpretation is correct, then these two pieces offer unique evidence that it was the practice in Antwerp, as in certain other cities, for a goldsmith to engage a specialist for this highly skilled work.

This ewer and basin also illustrate the typical dependence of the goldsmiths at this time on the artist-designer for much of the inspiration. Renaissance silver plate was judged on the profusion and variety of its surface ornament, and this element was usually supplied not by the goldsmith but by the leading court painters – for example, Giulio Romano at the Gonzaga court at Mantua, or Rosso at François I's court at Fontainebleau, or, in England, Hans Holbein at the court of Henry VIII. Vasari, in his account of Rosso, refers to 'the numberless designs that Rosso made for salt-cellars, vases, bowls, and other things of fancy, all of which the King afterwards caused to be executed in silver but these were so numerous that it would take too long to mention them all. Let it suffice to say that he made designs for all the vessels of a sideboard for the King'. Of course, there may have been one or two exceptions, like Benvenuto Cellini or Wenzel Jamnitzer, but even these outstandingly talented goldsmiths, who commanded the respect of kings and emperors, were frequently expected to work to the designs of a court artist. When in 1528 Cellini went to Mantua, the Duke Federigo Gonzaga commissioned him to make a reliquary and instructed Giulio Romano, his court painter, to supply the design for it. According to the bragging Cellini, whose autobiography frequently fails to distinguish fact from fiction, Giulio replied: 'My Lord, Benvenuto is a man who has no need of other people's sketches, as your Excellency will be able to judge when you see his model.' Similarly, when Wenzel Jamnitzer was summoned by the Emperor to Vienna in 1556 and received a major commission from the Archduke Ferdinand of Tirol for a large centre-piece or table-fountain, it was Jacopo da Strada who was nominated to be the designer. Furthermore, he suggested that he should supply not only the drawings but also a model of the fountain – and the accounts show that the Archduke rewarded him handsomely.

Many of these designs by the leading court artists were subsequently engraved and published during the sixteenth century so that they became available for all to copy. The workshops of the goldsmiths in every city in Europe were stocked with these engravings, but not every engraver made proper acknowledgement to his source and, consequently, the true authorship of these designs is often controversial. At least one of these engravers, Erasmus Hornick, was trained as a goldsmith, but because no single piece of silver can be identified as his work, it has been conjectured that he was a

Fig.47 'Water' and 'Piety': two silver-gilt tazze from the set of 12, embossed and chased with the Four Elements and the Eight Virtues. From the collection of the Counts von Thun of Tirol and Bohemia. Maker's mark, PH (in monogram) for Paul Hübner. Augsburg, end of 16th century. H. 5⅝ in (14.3 cm); diam. 8⅛ in (20.6 cm).

decorator and embosser of plate produced by other goldsmiths such as we saw in Figs.44–6. A complete set of twelve silver-gilt tazze (Fig.47) – in itself a most remarkable survival – is embossed with plaquette-like reliefs of the Four Elements and the Eight Virtues, all based on engravings but drawn from a number of different sources, including Jost Amman's *Kunstbuchlein*, which was first published in Frankfurt in 1578. None of the twelve tazze is dated but they were made in Augsburg by a leading goldsmith, Paul Hübner (master in 1583 – died in 1614), though oddly one bears the mark of Raimond Laminit. The elegant but extreme *contraposto* of the figures, the restless detail of the foreground and the handling of the landscapes that stretch far into the distance are florid aspects of the Late Mannerist style of Northern Europe.

Virtuosity was never more valued than at the courts of the Renaissance princes; indeed, the facility to achieve, with apparent ease, a *tour de force* and to overcome all the technical difficulties with sophisticated taste was the hallmark of Mannerism. A silver hand-bell in the Bequest (Colour Pl. XIIIA), entirely covered with all manner of reptiles, insects, shells, moss and foliage, is one such piece, a veritable *tour de force*, for each creature and each plant was cast in silver from nature and applied without any subsequent chasing or chiselled work. This brilliant demonstration of technical virtuosity is the work of the German goldsmith, Wenzel Jamnitzer, whose name ranks with Cellini. Born in Vienna in 1508, he was only eight years younger than Cellini, and, like Cellini, he served the most powerful princes of his day: four Hapsburg Emperors, the Archduke Ferdinand of Tirol, the Duke of Brunswick and the Chancellor of Bohemia were among his patrons, and yet, ironically, of their numerous important and monumental commissions almost nothing has survived. However, as a young man, Wenzel Jamnitzer had come to Nuremberg, where in 1534 he was granted citizenship and after ten years was made coin and seal-die cutter to the City – his first official appointment – and his most magnificent work to have survived is, in fact, the great centre-piece which the Nuremberg City Council bought from him in 1549. It remained in Nuremberg until the auction sale of the City silver in 1806; today it is in the Rijksmuseum, Amsterdam. On various parts of this spectacular work representing Mother Earth and her fruitfulness, Jamnitzer has profusely applied silver casts of tiny creatures, grasses and flowers, all taken from nature. This incredible technique was one of his many gifts that earned him the admiration of his contemporaries, for, as his friend Johann Neudorfer observed, the 'flowers and grasses are so delicate and thin that they move when one blows on them'.

These castings of natural phenomena, often tiny and fragile, are among the more eccentric manifestations of Mannerism within this medium, and items like this bell remained a continuous source of amazement for successive generations, even though the rightful identity of their creator had already been lost by the eighteenth century. In 1772, when Horace Walpole became the excited, proud owner of this silver bell, he wrote: '. . . wish me joy, I have changed all my Roman medals of great brass . . . for the uniquest thing in the world, a silver bell for an inkstand made by Benvenuto Cellini. It makes one believe all the extravagant encomiums he bestows on himself: indeed, so does his Perseus. Well, my bell is in the finest taste, and is swarmed by caterpillars, lizards, grasshoppers, flies and masques, that you would take it for one of the plagues of Egypt. They are all in *altissimo*, nay, in *outissimo relievo*, and yet almost invisible but with a glass. Such foliage, such fruitage.' Walpole had, in fact, obtained it from Lord Rockingham in the way he described and was no doubt aware that formerly it had been for a long time in Italy, in the collection of the Marquis Leonati of Parma. He clearly did not know that Wenzel Jamnitzer had made another silver bell of similar design but less richly encrusted with animal ornamentation, which was one of the treasures of the Dukes of Bavaria nor that Jamnitzer had received in 1558 from the Emperor Ferdinand I the very large sum of 54 gulden for a silver table-bell.

In that age of discovery, bizarre freaks of nature and exotic rarities, like ostrich eggs, nautilus shells, variegated minerals, or strange nuts from distant islands in the Indian Ocean, held a powerful fascination for these princely patrons of the Renaissance. These 'curiosities' would be given to the goldsmith, who, with boundless ingenuity, would create around them some fanciful work of art, half-sculptural, half-functional, but wholly intended to amaze and delight. The Bequest has many splendid examples of these whimsical conceits and among the earliest is the nautilus-shell cup (Colour Pl. XIIIB) made in Antwerp, probably in 1555–6. The anonymous goldsmith has combined imaginative invention with great technical skill, creating a sculptural stem composed of a Neptune astride a fantastic sea-monster half emerging from a large shell, while at the summit a second Neptune, brandishing a spear, rides on a sea-horse supported by the waves that seem to issue from the fish at the back. Since antiquity these nautilus shells from the Pacific and Indian Oceans have been treasured in Europe and often accredited with quasi-magical powers. Immensely sensuous with a flowing curvilinear outline and soft lustrous surface, the nautilus shell was the perfect marvel of nature for a Renaissance collector, because it also possessed an extraordinary natural construction of many compartments within. The almost mathematical precision of their relationship to each other excited the curiosity of those with a sense of scientific enquiry and caused amazement among the rest.

The Bequest has several cups made of other rare exotic materials, of which the ostrich-egg cup, with silver-gilt mounts bearing the hallmark of the City of Prague (Colour Pl. XIIIB), is perhaps one of the most attractively proportioned. In this example, made towards the end of the sixteenth century, the stem has been given a naturalistic form, with a lizard, a squirrel and an enamelled tortoise climbing over the vine-covered tree-trunk. Less beautiful, but of far greater 'curiosity' value, is the table-fountain (Colour Pl. XIIIB) formed from one half of a palm-nut that grows in the Seychelles Islands in the Indian Ocean. The pair to this scent-fountain, using the other half of the nut, is in the Kunsthistorisches Museum in Vienna, but regrettably neither is hallmarked, especially as each is individually decorated.

Today it is difficult for us to realise the tremendous fascination of these strange phenomena from newly discovered distant lands, but the fragments of rock brought back from the moon's surface in recent years have awakened a similar kind of reaction. We can gain an accurate impression of their extreme rarity value from the history of another similar Seychelles palm-nut, which is also preserved in the Kunsthistorisches Museum in Vienna; it was a gift from the Prince of Bantam in Java to the Dutch Admiral, Wolfer Hermannszen, in 1602 and, on his return to Europe, the Admiral sold it for the large sum of 4,000 guilders to the Emperor Rudolf II, who had his court goldsmith, Anton Schweinberger, create for it one of the most magnificent Late Mannerist settings in silver gilt to have survived. This Augsburg goldsmith, who was appointed to the *Kaiserliche Hofwerkstatt* at Prague in 1587 at the monthly salary of 10 guilders, died in 1603 shortly after completing this masterpiece, in which he has brilliantly transformed a tropical palm-nut into a work of art of great aesthetic merit. The unknown goldsmith who created the example in the Waddesdon Bequest and its companion piece in Vienna has provided beautifully embossed and chased silver-gilt mounts of a more conventional and restrained design that probably date from the third quarter of the sixteenth century – indeed, they may be the earliest silver-mounted Seychelles nuts to have survived.

The Waddesdon Bequest is exceptionally rich in tall standing-cups of silver gilt, mainly from the workshops of Augsburg and Nuremberg goldsmiths. These tall cups were increasingly in demand during the sixteenth century, either to be used as *Wilkomm* ('Welcome') cups or as presentation cups. Every guild, society and similar institution in Germany had a large 'Welcome' cup in which to drink the health of distinguished guests, and many noble castles and merchant houses kept a *Wilkomm* in the hall. Similarly, the custom of presenting every visitor of rank and importance with a tall cup of silver spread from the courts through to the cities and towns, until not only the German civic authorities but also the guilds and the leading patrician families were following suit.

Typical of the conventional standing-cup and cover, which the goldsmiths of Nuremberg favoured in the middle of the sixteenth century, is the pair (Fig.48) apparently made in 1568 for the well-known Nuremberg patrician, Leonhart Tucher, who died at the age of eighty-one in that year. Most of the decoration in relief on these cups is cast, including the elaborate cylindrical band on the drum; however, the intricate arabesque patterns below the lip and on the foot of the two cups is finely etched. The goldsmith, Christoph Lindenberger (master in 1546, died in 1580), was probably rather conservative, for in the design of this pair of cups he is still following the Renaissance canons of proportions and stressing the horizontal lines of the structure; the cups are not tall nor is there anything Mannerist about them except for certain details of the surface ornament.

Rather more Mannerist in style is a silver-gilt cup and cover of similar size (Fig.49), which was probably made in Germany during the third quarter of the sixteenth

Fig. 48 One of a pair of silver-gilt standing-cups and covers; cast ornament on the drum with finely etched mauresques on lip, base and on the foot. Maker's mark for Christoph Lindenberger. Nuremberg, c.1568. H. 10 in (25.4 cm).

Fig. 49 Silver-gilt standing-cup and cover of unusual form reminiscent of the engraved designs by Matthias Zundt and Virgil Solis produced in Nuremberg in the 1550s. Embossed, chased and enriched with translucent enamelling. Mark illegible; probably Nuremberg, third quarter of 16th century. H. 10¼ in (26 cm).

century. The bowl is embossed with fourteen lobes and rests on a cushion-like base, ornamented with chased lozenge network, whilst the stem is decorated with caryatid satyrs, goats' heads and sea-horses. This cup is an interesting example of the rare use of translucent enamelling (sapphire, green and ruby) to enrich the surface of the silver. This enamel, being fired, has survived in a fairly good condition, though the red enamel has somewhat decayed. Indeed, it has been suggested that many more pieces of German sixteenth-century silver were originally coloured – not with fired enamel but with *kaltemail* (a kind of hard-setting paint that was applied cold). The latter has, in most cases, disappeared over the years, and only in a few cases are traces of colour still to be found; if this was, indeed, the practice, then our present assessment and appreciation of the plainer items may not be historically accurate.

By the end of the sixteenth century, the German standing-cup and cover had changed its proportions, increasing its height without any corresponding widening of its form. These elongated shapes were far more in keeping with Mannerist taste, and the new designs tended to give them a more continuous integrated flow from the foot-rim to the finial, so that the separate elements of cover, bowl, stem and foot began to disappear. The goldsmith who most successfully introduced these new ideas was Hans Petzolt, who, after Wenzel Jamnitzer, is the most famous of the Nuremberg goldsmiths of the sixteenth century. The Bequest contains two of his splendid creations (Colour Pl. xv), both dating from the end of the century.

Petzolt, who was twenty-seven when he was admitted a master in 1578, lived a very active life until his death in 1633. Like Wenzel Jamnitzer, he became a member of the *Grosse Rat* or grand council of the City and played an active role in civic affairs. Although he was summoned to Prague by the Emperor Rudolf II on more than one occasion, Petzolt, in his workshop in Nuremberg, was chiefly concerned with the production of these presentation cups, which the City Council, in particular, commissioned and purchased from him in astonishing numbers. Because so many of them went straight into the *Schatzkammern* of monarchs and powerful nobles, a higher proportion of his work has survived than of any of his contemporaries.

Of the two monumental cups by Hans Petzolt in the Bequest, the slightly smaller one (Colour Pl. xv) illustrates his early attempt to combine Renaissance and Late Gothic silver forms and decorative motifs. He went on to produce many cups with these protruding bosses and petal-like lobes in the Late Gothic style, but, in this cup, Hans Petzolt's attempts to unify the design by making the foot echo the design of the body have been marred by the old-fashioned Renaissance baluster stem with its three scroll brackets, which remains obtrusively distinct and separate.

In the other cup (Colour Pl. xv), which is on a monumental scale, Hans Petzolt has achieved a far more integrated design – so much so that even the join of the cover is completely disguised by the continuous design of the bunch of grapes. This form of cup is listed in contemporary inventories as a *Traubenpokal* (that is, 'a bunch of grapes cup'), though it is now generally known as a 'pineapple cup' (quite erroneously). Although reminiscent of the general style of German silver cups around 1500, no Late Gothic example of this form is known and, indeed, the design may have been the invention of Hans Petzolt himself. He is known to have supplied the City of Nuremberg alone with eighteen *Traubenpokale*, and each may have been made to a different and highly individual design. Certainly, several of Petzolt's finest versions of the *Traubenpokal*, usually with a human figure forming the stem, have survived; in the example in the

Kunstgewerbemuseum, Berlin, the stem takes the form of the Emperor clad in armour with shield and spear, whilst in the Bequest it takes the form of a nude Bacchus. Both are well modelled and both demonstrate Petzolt's ambition to emulate Wenzel Jamnitzer, whose sculptural achievements in silver were so outstandingly effective and greatly admired.

Other presentation cups made by Hans Petzolt and his contemporaries in Nuremberg demonstrate even more vividly the extent to which Late Gothic silver forms were being faithfully echoed, so much so that they are generally described as *Neugotik* and regarded as part of the Gothic revival that occurred during the first half of the seventeenth century in Northern Europe. In the Bequest, this neo-Gothic style is best exemplified by a tall cup (Colour Pl. xv) made by Michael Müller, who did not become a master until 1612 and died in 1650. This cup, with its bold twisted gadroons and tapering elegance terminating in the figure of the Pope, was probably made during the second or third decade of the century, when this Gothicising trend was reaching its peak and when the effects of the Counter-Reformation were beginning to be felt.

It has been suggested that this harking back to the Late Gothic styles of pre-Reformation times may, therefore, have been more than a mere stylistic preference on the part of Hans Petzolt and his fellow goldsmiths in Nuremberg, although it did undoubtedly coincide with a tremendous revival of interest in Dürer, fostered to some extent by the Emperor Rudolf ii's own personal enthusiasm for this artist. Dürer had been born in Nuremberg in 1471, the son of a goldsmith, and had at first been trained as a goldsmith; indeed, his early designs for silver made soon after 1500 include some of the loveliest versions of these Late Gothic lobed and gadrooned cups. As the cult of Dürer gathered momentum towards the end of the sixteenth century, it was perhaps inevitable that the Nuremberg goldsmiths should go back to his designs and seek inspiration in them. Whilst Hans Petzolt and some of his more gifted contemporaries succeeded in doing so without losing their own touch of originality, others like Jacob Stoer were less able. The design of his standing-cup and cover in the Waddesdon Bequest (Colour Pl. xv) echoes the work of Hans Petzolt, but the embossed and chased ornament, with its trophies of fish and its birds in arabesques, is lacking vitality and originality. Jacob Stoer did not become a master until 1626 and was dead before 1660, and his work, as exemplified by this competently executed standing-cup and cover, typifies the malaise that had befallen the goldsmiths of Nuremberg. In the end, this nostalgic backward-looking policy seems to have had a stultifying effect on their craft and perhaps even to have contributed to the gradual decline of Nuremberg during the seventeenth century, while its great rival, Augsburg, steadily rose to become the major centre for goldsmiths in Southern Germany.

Exhibiting none of these symptoms of decline is the fine, early seventeenth-century Nuremberg ewer and basin (Figs.50,51) of Johann Moritz von Nassau-Siegen (1604–79), Governor of Brazil (1636–46), and Stadtholder of the Duchy of Cleves (1647–79). These two historic pieces of plate entered the collection of Baron Anselm Rothschild in Vienna only because the Reformed Church in Cleves in 1869, after 204 years of faithful guardianship, decided to sell them. Johann Moritz, who had been Stadtholder for eighteen years when he gave them to the Church in 1665, was anxious that they should be used for christenings because he was aware that they had been purchased by his parents with money that had been sent on the occasion of his own christening in 1604 by the most illustrious of his godparents, Maurice, Prince of Orange and Count of Nassau. The latter had succeeded as Stadtholder of Holland, Utrecht and Zeeland upon the assassination of his father, William the Silent, in 1584 and, like most of the other distinguished godparents, Prince Maurice could not attend the christening in Cleves in 1604 because of the war being fought in the Netherlands against the Spanish. As Dr Johann ter Molen has recently shown, the archives record that the very large sum of money sent by Prince Maurice as a christening present was immediately transferred to Amsterdam to pay for the military expenses of the two half-brothers of the newborn babe, both of whom were in the service of the States-General. A document of 1610 records that the money had, indeed, been used for purposes other than the purchase of christening plate and that the position had still to be rectified. How long elapsed after 1610 before action was taken is still not known, but by 1625 matters had been put right because an inventory of plate belonging to Johann Moritz's widowed mother included 'A large dish with the coat of arms of Orange with its ewer, which His Excellency, Prince Maurice, had presented'.

Between 1610 and 1625 this ewer and basin had been supplied by a Nuremberg goldsmith. His stamp was a B but his identity remains uncertain, though it seems likely that he could have been one of three masters, Hieronymous Berckhauser (born in 1567, master in 1598), Hans Bauch the Younger (master in 1595) or Heinrich Brinckmann (master in 1599). The circular basin has a central boss, set with a silver medallion ($2\frac{1}{2}$ in, 6.2 cm diameter) with a silver-gilt frame, partly plain and partly tooled to resemble a wire chain. This armorial medallion, which was made separately, is engraved, partly gilded and partly enamelled in blue, black and traces of green, with the coat of arms, three crests and mantling of Maurice, Prince of Orange and Count of Nassau (1566–1625), surmounted by the engraved letters, MPZVGZN (Moritz Prinz zu Uranien Graf zu Nassau). Curiously, the date, 1604, which is engraved and enamelled in black beneath the shield, has not previously been noticed or recorded, but close examination indicates that it is original and not a modern addition.

The basin (Fig.52), which is ornamented with concentric bands of varying widths and differing embossed and chased designs, has in its broad bottom three reserved panels containing Old Testament scenes of salvation through Divine intervention: firstly, Daniel seated in the Lions' Den with a figure emerging from the clouds; secondly, Jonah being cast up by the whale; and thirdly, an unidentified scene of a young man, almost nude, seated on a sea-shore, apparently being attacked by two animals, perhaps lions (on the right), and two dolphins or whales (on the left), whilst the Hand of God emerges from the clouds and grasps the young man's upraised arm. Among the various possible identifications that have been suggested by Dr ter Molen and others, perhaps the most likely is Isaiah, 42: 5–6:

Thus saith God the Lord, he that created the heavens, and stretched them out; he that spread forth the earth, and that which cometh out of it; he that giveth bread unto the people upon it and spirit to them that walk herein:
I the Lord have called thee in righteousness, and will hold thine hand, and will keep thee, and give thee for a covenant of the people . . .

The band of formal ornament on the steep sides of the basin and the broader band on the flat rim, with its winged cherub heads in high relief and garlands of fruit within a subdued form of strap-work, are part of the repertoire of Nuremberg goldsmiths in the early seventeenth-century. The present appearance of the basin scarcely differs from

Fig. 50 (*Below*) Silver-gilt ewer made *en suite* with basin (Fig. 51) and together purchased between 1610 and 1625 with the money sent by Prince Maurice of Orange on the occasion of the christening of Johann Moritz von Nassau-Siegen (1604–79) at Cleves. Maker's mark, B; Nuremberg town mark, first quarter of 17th century.

Fig. 53 (*Below*) Lithograph, published in 1857, of the ewer and basin which was presented in 1665 by Johann Moritz von Nassau-Siegen to the Reformed Church in Cleves. It proves that the ewer changed its shape and form after the Church had sold the ewer and basin in 1869 and before it entered Baron Anselm's collection in Vienna.

Fig. 51 Silver-gilt basin accompanying the ewer (Fig. 50); in the centre, a medallion dated 1604 and enamelled with the arms of Prince Maurice of Orange (1566–1625), the most illustrious of the godparents of Johann Moritz. Maker's mark, B; Nuremberg town mark, first quarter of the 17th century. Diam. 22⅜ in (56.8 cm).

Fig. 52 One of three cartouches on the basin (Fig. 51), each embossed and chased with an Old Testament scene of deliverance from disaster through Divine intervention. The tentative identity of the subject of this panel with *Isaiah*, 42: 5–6, has yet to be confirmed.

Fig. 54 (*Above*) Detail of the
upper part of the ewer
(Fig. 50), which was added
after 1869. The scene of
Samson and Delilah closely
resembles a print by
Matthaeus Merian
produced in 1626; no earlier
version has yet been
discovered.

Fig. 55 (*Right*) Detail of the
front of the ewer (Fig. 50)
where an embossed mask is
incorporated into the design
and covers the hole where
the spout had been prior to
1869.

its original condition, though three holes remain on the underside to testify to the way in which a later silver foot had been added. This foot was removed after 1869 and is now lost.

The ewer was made *en suite* with the basin but its unique and curious form is due to a fundamental remodelling of the ewer, which was carried out after the sale in 1869. Fortunately, the ewer and basin were engraved by T. O. Wrigel in Leipzig and published in a lithograph, together with a full description in 1857 (Ernst aus'm Weerth, *Kunstdenkmäler des Christlichen Mittelalters in den Rheinlanden*, Leipzig, 1857, Pl. IX). By comparing the lithograph of 1857 (Fig.53) with the ewer, it becomes clear that a number of significant alterations took place immediately after 1869; firstly, the cover surmounted by a lion holding a shield has disappeared; secondly, in place of the cover, an upper zone of a slightly cushion-shape form tapering to a narrow neck has been added; thirdly, the spout, which in the lithograph is shown projecting almost horizontally from the shoulder of the ewer just below the rim, has been removed and joined to the top of the neck at an almost vertical angle though, fortunately, it still bears the two stamps (the maker's mark and the Nuremberg town mark); fourthly, the exceptionally fine handle has been detached from the body of the ewer (as shown in the lithograph) and fastened to the top of the slender neck and to the shoulder of the cushion-shape zone; fifthly, the holes in the body of the ewer left by the removal of the spout and the handle have been so skilfully filled in and embossed with a cherub's head and a grotesque mask that the 'filling-in' can scarcely be detected with the naked eye.

The remaining embossed decoration on the sides of the ewer comprises two large oval panels, surrounded by a variety of Mannerist ornamental motifs: in one panel, a standing female figure with a falcon on her extended hand and an anchor by her feet represents 'Hope'; the other panel contains the figure of 'Temperance', depicted holding a ewer in her raised left hand and a tazza in her other hand. Both compositions derive ultimately from designs by Goltzius, made familiar by the engravings of Jakob Matham, but may have been copied from near-contemporary plaquettes.

The upper zone and narrow neck, which were added immediately following the sale in 1869, are embossed in a most convincingly similar style with fruit swags and two oval reserved panels enclosing scenes from the story of Samson: the slaying of the Philistines with a jaw-bone of an ass, and Delilah cutting off Samson's hair (Fig.54). In his recent account of the Dutch sources, Dr ter Molen has shown that both compositions follow closely the engravings in the Bible produced by Matthaeus Merian in 1630, which were first issued by Merian in 1626 in a series of Biblical prints he had created. Whereas his engraving of the *Slaying of the Philistines* repeats in many respects the print by Cornelius Metsys dated 1549, the *Samson and Delilah* composition is thought by Dr ter Molen to be Merian's own invention in 1625–6.

If this opinion is correct and no engraved source was available until 1626, the upper zone of the ewer cannot have been made before 1626, that is to say, after the ewer and basin were listed in the 1625 inventory. The upper zone must, therefore, either have formed part of another silver-gilt object of the second quarter of the seventeenth century and in 1869, when the ewer was being refashioned, been cut out and added to the ewer or, alternatively, it must have been the special creation of a goldsmith in 1869, deliberately copying the Merian engravings and working in the manner of the Nuremberg goldsmiths of about 1620, in order to create a harmonious addition to the rest of the ewer. If it is the work of a modern goldsmith about 100 years ago, it is a

Fig. 56 Silver-gilt huntsman with detachable head. Maker's mark for Christoff Ritter; Nuremberg town mark, late 16th century. H.12 in (30.5 cm).

Fig. 57 Clockwork movement of steel, mounted on wheels, from the base of the table-ornament (Fig. 56); designed to propel the figure along the table. Nuremberg, late 16th century.

remarkable essay in imitation of the early seventeenth-century Nuremberg masters and deserves close study. Certainly, the skill with which the three holes in the body have been filled (Fig.55) lends support to this latter interpretation, but why a goldsmith in 1869 should choose to copy the Merian engravings of these two scenes remains a mystery.

Before turning to look at some of the later German silver in the Bequest, attention must be drawn to the rare sixteenth-century examples of small-scale sculpture in silver. Two of the finest were made in Nuremberg, and the earlier (Fig.56) is both a table-ornament and an amusing toy, designed to move along the table propelled by the clockwork mechanism hidden in the base. It represents a huntsman in the fashionable attire of the late sixteenth century, accompanied by his dog and poised ready to spear the boar. The gilded figure of the huntsman contrasts with the oval silver base, which is encrusted with fern-like branches and lizards in full relief, reminiscent of Wenzel Jamnitzer's work on the silver bell (Colour Pl. XIIIA). The maker of this table-ornament was Christoff Ritter, one of the more prominent goldsmiths of Nuremberg, who became master in 1547 and in 1551 supplied the Municipality with a handsome salt. Though the original iron clockwork movement in the base (Fig.57) has, by good fortune, survived, its maker cannot be identified at present.

The other Nuremberg figure (Colour Pl. XIVA), which is also partly gilded, was clearly never intended to be mechanised, since it has been designed without any base at all. As a work of sculpture, however, this figure of a peasant gathering grapes is far superior to the huntsman. A tense realism and strong characterisation of this virile subject has been most skilfully accomplished by the talented goldsmith Elias Lencker, who must have made this figure after he had become master in 1562 and before his death in 1591. Few silver figures of comparable quality have survived to testify to the remarkably high standards of the contemporaries of Jamnitzer and Petzolt in Nuremberg in its heyday. In Dresden, in the Grünes Gewölbe, there is still to be seen one of Elias Lencker's finest surviving creations, the magnificent *Calvary* of 1577, which may have been made for the Electress Anna and which was subsequently placed in the Elector of Saxony's Cabinet of Curiosities. With its tall, slender, elongated Crucifix seeming to float above the hill of nautilus shells, large irregular pearls, turquoises, emeralds, garnets, and a myriad of tiny reptiles cast in silver from nature, Elias Lencker has combined technical virtuosity with originality of design, whilst in the figure of Christ and in the six reliefs of scenes from the Passion (on the pedestal), he has demonstrated his great artistic abilities – regrettably, only a small proportion of his *oeuvre* seems to have survived.

The Bequest also contains one very striking demonstration of the level of excellence and wealth of patronage being maintained during the late sixteenth century at the three main centres of the goldsmiths' craft in Northern Germany – Lübeck, Lüneburg and Hamburg. It is a tall flagon with hinged cover (Fig.58) and, contrary to the normal design, narrows towards the high foot. This distinctive form is usually known as a *Hansekanne* because of its popularity with the wealthy merchants of the many towns belonging to the Hanseatic League, a famous political and commercial organisation of Northern Germanic towns created in 1241; the form appears to have been developed in the Baltic region and to have been made at all the major centres from Hamburg in the west to Riga in the east.

The flagon in the Bequest was made around 1600 in Lübeck by a goldsmith using the mark of a rose, who has been identified as Englebrecht Becker II. It is undoubtedly one of the finest and most elaborate examples to have survived – and, of course, only a few isolated pieces outside Lübeck have been preserved, for the destruction of Lübeck silver belonging to the City and the guilds has been extremely thorough over the last 200 years. This flagon appears to have survived because it had become part of the official plate of the City of Riga by 1622, for, like the wonderful *Hansekanne* by Dirich Utermarke, preserved in the Statens Historiska Museum, Stockholm, it bears the arms of Riga and the date added inside the cover.

Another very similar flagon from Lübeck has survived in the Kremlin, in Moscow; it was made by Klaus Wiese, who became master in 1567 and died in 1612. Like the Waddesdon Bequest flagon, it is partially gilt and enriched with engraved and embossed ornament. It has a band of pierced openwork applied around the cylindrical body, an elaborate thumb-piece and, most characteristic of all, a richly decorated handle broken, as it were, by a disc-like button and terminating in the most profuse spiral tendrils at the end of which are ball-shaped flowers or fruit. A slightly less ornate version made in Hamburg in 1588 is among the earliest-dated examples to have survived; it was formerly in the Rothschild collection in Frankfurt and was acquired in 1968 by the Museum für Kunst und Gewerbe in Hamburg. Indeed, towards the end of the sixteenth century the importance of both Lüneberg and Lübeck as centres of the craft dwindled and Hamburg became supreme, winning for itself the powerful patronage of the courts of Denmark and Sweden.

A silver-gilt cup in the Bequest (Fig.59), surmounted by the bust of Gustavus Adolphus, King of Sweden (1594–1632), serves as a vivid reminder of the great tragedy that befell Europe, particularly many of those Germanic cities that lay between the Baltic and the Danube, during the Thirty Years War (1618–48). This cup is one of several made in the North German city of Frankfurt-am-Main by a goldsmith of that city, Paul Birckenholtz. He died in 1633, but in the preceding years he produced several of these cups to celebrate the achievements of the hero of the Protestant North, Gustavus Adolphus. Heavily subsidised by Cardinal Richelieu of France, the Swedish King had landed in 1630 in Germany and led his Lutheran forces, in the spirit of crusaders, southwards against the imperial might of the Catholic Hapsburgs, seizing Mainz and then Munich itself. From there he marched on Vienna. At the Battle of Lutzen in November 1632, the Swedes, hampered by fog, permitted their King, charging with reckless fury, to become encircled by the enemy beyond his own lines; he fell from his wounded horse and was shot in the nape of the neck by a cavalryman. His death was a disaster and his army soon withdrew to the Baltic. The majority of Lutheran princes began negotiations for peace but the intervention of France kept the war going for another fifteen years, during which time armies marched and counter-marched across Germany, bringing havoc and destruction to many parts.

The silver-gilt cup in the Bequest is decorated around the bowl with applied figures of the Virtues, two in each of the four roundels, and on the foot are four groups of military trophies whilst, inside the cover, a tablet is engraved with a eulogy of the King in sixteen lines of verse. The stem of the cup is in the form of a heraldic lion rampant armed with sword and buckler – most appropriate for so tireless a warrior king.

Heraldic beasts and certain other animals were popular forms in which to fashion standing silver-gilt cups, and, though relatively few have survived, the Bequest is particularly rich in these handsome creatures, especially those of the chase – the stag,

Fig.58 (*Far right*) Silver-gilt covered flagon; the pierced and embossed decoration includes a hunting scene (continuing below the handle). Maker's mark for Englebrecht Becker II; Lubeck town mark, *c*.1600. H. 15¼ in (38.7 cm).

Fig.59 (*Right*) Silver-gilt standing-cup and cover in celebration of Gustavus Adolphus, King of Sweden (1594–1632); a lengthy eulogy of him in verse engraved on a silver tablet (inside the cover). Made by Paul Birckenholtz in Frankfurt-am-Main, *c*.1630. H. 13¾ in (35 cm).

the boar and the bear. Four were made in Augsburg, one in Vienna and, of the two made in Nuremberg, the finer is unquestionably the unicorn rampart by Heinrich Jonas, who was master in 1579 and died in 1605 (Fig.60). The modelling of the unicorn is sensitive and far more lively than in many of these heraldic representations. As is normal on these cups, the head is detachable and may have served as a drinking-cup. On the chest of the unicorn are two enamelled shields of arms, one of which includes the armorial bearing of a *unicorn rampant or*; no doubt this cup was made for the head of the family towards the end of the sixteenth century.

Cups of this kind were wrought in whatever form was most applicable for the recipient or patron – cups made for a guild would express the activity of that guild, like

Fig.60 Silver-gilt standing-cup in the form of a unicorn rampant standing on a domed base with silver lizards, snails, tortoises and toads, all cast in full relief. Maker's mark for Heinrich Jonas; Nuremberg town mark, late 16th century. H.13in (33cm).

Fig. 61 Silver-gilt cup of foliate form with a vine leaf forming the cover and three smiths hammering at an anvil forming a sculptural stem. Maker's mark for Marx Weinold; Augsburg town mark, *c.* 1690. H. 16¾ in (42.5 cm).

Fig. 62 Silver-gilt covered cup or vase commemorating the Siege of Freiberg in Saxony in 1643; set with many painted enamel plaques recording the historic events of the Siege. Made by Samuel Klemm, Freiberg, 1670. H. 19⅝ in (49.8 cm).

a shoe for the Shoemakers' Guild, and cups made for a nobleman might take the form of his heraldic crest or a prominent feature of his armorial bearings. One of the few fully documented examples of this practice is the magnificently realistic silver-gilt cup of a snail issuing forth from its shell, which was presented in 1564 to an exclusive Society of Nobles who used to meet at the Sign of the Snail, a house next to the Town Hall in Zurich. It still belongs to the Society but is deposited on loan to the Swiss National Museum in Zurich. It was made in Augsburg by a member of the Hueter family and presented to the Society by the Zurich merchant, Georg Albrecht; were it not for these incontrovertible facts, this cup might be regarded today as merely another curious demonstration of Mannerist art and its obsession with such forms. It was the custom in most guilds and societies in Germany for members to present silver cups on their appointment to an official position and, of course, this practice, combined with the customary rivalry between the guilds and the admiration of virtuosity, led to the production of some highly ostentatious and elaborate creations, such as the very tall cup in the Bequest (Fig.61). This cup, made in Augsburg, is not only surmounted by a small figure of a smith but actually has incorporated within the design of its stem an anvil, around which are standing and hammering three more smiths, and in front of the anvil is a painted enamel medallion with a coat of arms and the inscription: 'Adam Schmidt, 1690'. The ornate style of this cup, with its thin crinkled leaf motifs and richly embossed surface decoration, is typical of Augsburg baroque goldsmiths' work towards the end of the seventeenth century. In addition to the Augsburg hallmark, this cup bears a maker's mark, MW, the stamp of Marx Weinold, who died in 1700.

Perhaps the most eccentric piece of baroque silver in the Bequest is the huge vase and cover of silver gilt (Fig.62), made in 1670 to commemorate the Siege of Freiberg, in Saxony, in 1643 and the prowess of the Colonel of the Guard, Wolf Friedrich Muffels von Ermreuth. The vase is set with numerous small plaques of painted enamel, each depicting, on a white ground, a colourful scene from the events of the Siege; above each of these miniature paintings is an enamelled plaque with an inscription explaining the event being portrayed. This historic piece of plate, with its curious pictorial record executed in enamel, corresponds almost exactly to the working drawing and full description which survive in the library of the Society of Antiquaries of Freiberg. It was executed by a local goldsmith, Samuel Klemm, who became master in 1644, and although he was a good craftsman and a competent enameller, there is a naïvety and a provincialism about his handling of baroque forms and motifs, which, when compared with the works of the court goldsmiths, looks clumsy and gauche. Even Samuel Klemm's greatest surviving work, the ceremonial Miner's Outfit made for the Elector Johann Georg II between 1675 and 1677, lacks the quality of excellence achieved by the Dresden goldsmiths of the day. It was made for the Elector to wear during the processions and ceremonies of the Miners' Festival, which was intended to demonstrate the importance of mining to the prosperity of Saxony, and consequently, only semi-precious stones mined in Saxony were used to enrich the surface of the silver. Like the Siege of Freiberg vase and cover in the Bequest, the handles of the miner's axe and dagger, the scabbard of the sword and the lid of the purse are set with small enamel plaques painted with minute figural scenes and, again, enamelled inscriptions on adjacent enamel panels provide the explanatory information. Samuel Klemm was sixty-six when he finished the Miner's Outfit in 1677 and he died the following year; today, this magnificent achievement can be seen in the Grünes Gewölbe in Dresden.

8. Conclusion

In addition to these six main groups, the Bequest contains a number of objects of a highly disparate nature, many made for the courts of the sixteenth and seventeenth centuries. Maximilian I, Duke of Bavaria (1597–1651) and Electoral Prince (from 1623), was a great patron of the arts, who gathered at his court in Munich a small group of the best steel chisellers and armourers in Europe and created the Munich school, which reached and maintained for nearly 100 years the highest standards, both technically and artistically. By about 1590 Emmanuel Sadeler and his younger brother Daniel had settled in Munich, having come, it is thought, from the Southern Netherlands, probably from Antwerp, where their father may have been the bladesmith, Emmanuel de Sadeler. By 1600, the two brothers were well-established at the ducal court, and most of their finest work was either for the personal use of members of the Duke's family or as presentation pieces.

All their pieces are decorated by means of a brilliant technique that is particularly resistant to wear and, consequently, even today many of their works are in almost pristine condition. It consisted of chiselling the ornamental detail in blued steel – the natural colour of heated steel – and heavily gilding the surrounding metal. The contrast between the deep blue, with its fine ornamentation, and the rich gold was most effective and far more popular than the alternative method of applying silver to contrast with the gold, for the silver was soon rubbed and lost its appeal. Whereas in the past goldsmiths would have been called in to add the decorative embellishments in various precious metals on to the steel, the armourers of the Munich school, led by the Sadeler brothers, were able to carry out the whole operation themselves. For the ornamental designs, they drew upon the best engravings, either by artists of the Fontainebleau School, like Étienne Delaune, or Netherlandish and German engravers, like Hans Collaert (1540–1622).

Daniel, who lived until about 1633, when he appears to have died of the plague, is represented in the Bequest by a wheel-lock gun (Colour Pl. XIIA, Fig.63), which ranks beyond doubt as one of the finest firearms in existence. It was probably made about 1620, when an almost identical gun, now preserved in the Wallace Collection, London, was also produced. The barrels of both guns are decorated with three panels of finely chiselled ornament on blued steel against a gilded background; the subjects, mainly figures from classical mythology, are surrounded by floral scroll-work, grotesques and masks. Daniel Sadeler's source for these panels is undoubtedly Étienne Delaune; he has either copied directly from the engravings or been content to introduce a few minor modifications. The lock-plate is chased with a Triumph of Neptune, slight variants of which he used on a number of pieces. The stock, with its butt of modified fish-tail form (Fig. 64), has a restrained and sophisticated elegant appearance. Whereas snake-wood has been used to stock the gun in the Wallace Collection, which is signed by the stock-maker, Hieronymous Borstorffer, the gun in the Bequest is stocked in walnut. Both stocks are undoubtedly made by the same hand, and in each case the decoration of inlaid ivory comprises no more than a few strong lines following the contours of the stock and some extremely intricate scroll-work. Hieronymous Borstorffer seems to have been working in Munich from about 1595 until his death in 1637 and to have stocked many of the guns made by the Sadelers.

There is a Renaissance table-clock of uncertain origin in the Bequest (Figs.65,66), which has a movement that incorporates several features of special horological interest. The movement which undoubtedly dates from the second half of the sixteenth century, probably around 1570–80, may have been made in Spain or the Southern Netherlands. The trains, which are set at right angles to the dial, have undergone considerable alteration; the original alarum mechanism has been removed and the astronomical dial, together with the extra, under-dial gearing, has been added, probably in modern times, in imitation of the famous dial of the Piazza di San Marco in Venice. The clock was designed to strike the hours, and the method of securing the striking levers does not accord with the usual French or German practice at this date. Similarly, the method of fitting the fusee to the going-train is most unusual, though the same system is apparently used on the rather similar clock by Hans d'Evalo. This documentary piece was sent as a present to Japan in 1612 and has since been preserved in the Temple of Toshogu; it is signed: '*Hans de Valo me fecit en Madrid a 1581*'. Hans d'Evalo was an interesting maker, who was born in Brussels and in 1558 began forty years of service at the Spanish court, becoming clockmaker to King Philip II in 1580. There is a possibility that the clock in the Bequest was also made in Spain or the Southern Netherlands, either by this maker or in his workshop. The present rather

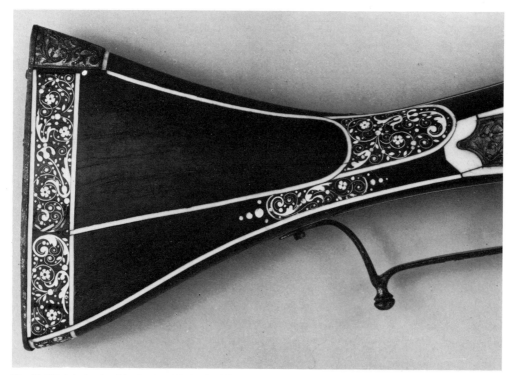

Fig. 63 (*Right*) A wheel-lock gun with finely chiselled ornament on blued steel against a gilded ground (see Colour Pl. XIIA). Made by Daniel Sadeler at the Bavarian court, Munich, *c*.1620. L. 68 in (172.7 cm).

Fig. 64 (*Above*) Detail of the butt of the gun (Fig.63), of walnut with inlaid ivory; made by the stock-maker, Hieronymous Borstorffer.

88

Venetian-looking exterior is misleading, for the nielli inscription and plaques of the Doges and Lion of St Mark are modern additions; the rest of the case, which was undoubtedly specially made to accommodate the unusual technical features of the movement, could well have been made in the late sixteenth century in a Spanish or Flemish workshop, though the lack of sufficient horological material of indisputable Spanish or Flemish origin makes the firm attribution of this interesting clock extremely difficult.

Cameos and engraved gems of the Renaissance are equally hard to attribute to specific artists and their workshops, though the names of many have been recorded. Gem-engraving was an art that blossomed in the Early Renaissance in Italy under the keen competition of assiduous collectors, like Pope Martin V (1417–31), Leonello d'Este of Ferrara (1407–50), Dandolo of Venice, Giustiniani of Genoa, Cardinal Francesco Gonzaga, Pope Paul II (1464–71) and, perhaps most eager of them all, Lorenzo de Medici (1449–92). These collectors purchased, often for large sums, the newly discovered engraved gems of classical Greece and Rome and, consequently, Italian workshops frequently produced copies with the intention of deceiving collectors. Long before the end of the fifteenth century, however, the works of many

contemporary Italian gem-engravers were highly prized as works of art in their own right.

The Bequest has several fine examples but perhaps the rarest are the twenty-two shell cameos, which are set not in jewellery but on a silver-gilt cup and cover (Colour Pl. xvi). Furthermore, these shell cameos were carved not in an Italian workshop but in France, probably in the first quarter of the sixteenth century. The subjects are almost all religious and, sometimes, are accompanied by French inscriptions, such as GENEVIEVE beside the figure of St Geneviève holding a book and a candle. The square cameo of Tobit, with his wallet and staff, bears the inscription PETIT THOBIE, whilst the companion cameo of the Archangel Gabriel is rhomboidal so that it will fit on to the cover of the cup along with six others. French inscriptions identify six other saints (SS. Margareta, Nicolas, Jaques, Bernart, Gregoire, Come and Damian), but a tonsured saint with a lance and a priest wearing a cape and holding a chalice have no inscription beside them. The square cameos of Our Lord, the Virgin Mary, the Devil, the Angel, and an executioner with raised sword are all readily recognisable. At least two of these cameos appear to be modern replacements, like the miniature silver figure on the apex of the cover of the cup. However, these rare cameos are very similar to a small group in the Cabinet des Médailles in Paris, three of which came from the Chasse of S. Geneviève, destroyed at the Mint in 1793. Other similar shell cameos with sacred and secular subjects are preserved in the Bargello in Florence, in the Museo Nazionale in Naples, on a 'house-altar' in the Bayerische Nationalmuseum, Munich, and in the Imperial collections in Vienna.

Fig.67 Drawing of a *nef* (or ship-salt) set with shell cameos (see Colour Pl. xvi); from the illuminated inventory of the Treasury at Halle (the *Hallesches Heiltumbuch*).

Perhaps most interestingly, two other silver-gilt covered cups set with comparable cameos have survived: one cup, attributed to Ludwig Krug of Nuremberg (c. 1488–1532), is in the Museum of Decorative Arts, Budapest, and the other is in the Treasury of the Basilica of San Antonio in Padua. A drawing of a similar covered cup inscribed with Ludwig Krug's name is in the *Hallesches Heiltumbuch* – an illuminated inventory of the Treasury at Halle made in 1526 – and on another page (fol. 367v) of this inventory is illustrated a silver-gilt salt in the form of a ship (or *nef*) ornamented with many small rectangular shell cameos of the very same kind (Fig.67). This 'ship-salt', formerly at Halle, has been attributed to Ludwig Krug, but some of the lesser silversmiths may have followed Krug's example and, while the fashion lasted, enriched their more conventionally designed cups with these shell cameos from France.

In the absence of any punch-marks, the precise origins of this covered cup and of similar German-looking silver cups of this early period, c. 1520–30, are difficult to identify. It is known, for example, that Ludwig's elder brother, Emil Krug, settled in Strasburg after his marriage in 1506 to a citizen of that city and, although no marked products of his Strasburg workshop have been recorded, there are one or two attributable works, including a pair of covered silver-gilt cups set with replicas of antique coins that were made for the Count of Alsace, Wilhelm Honstein, who became Bishop of Strasburg in 1506 and died in 1541. This powerful Prince-Bishop, who was highly regarded by both the Emperor Maximilian I and his successor, Charles V, conducting various diplomatic missions in their service, could have provided Emil Krug with the lavish style of patronage he needed, whilst Strasburg would have provided a meeting-point for French and German tastes.

Just as the art of carving shell has a long history going back to the classical world, so carved amber was used for decorative purposes in remote antiquity. However, it was during the seventeenth and early eighteenth centuries that the artistic and technical handling of amber reached a degree of perfection never before attained. Perhaps the very considerable limitations imposed by its physical properties made amber a worthy challenge for those gifted ivory carvers and talented craftsmen who were to make Königsberg, on the Baltic coast, famous for its school of amber carving. The works of Georg Schreiber and Jacob Heise in the middle decades of the seventeenth century are as finely carved and as artistically accomplished as their rivals in ivory or in rhinoceros horn. Perhaps with the destruction of the famous Amber Room at Tzarskoe-Selo during the Second World War, the Grünes Gewölbe in Dresden has become the richest collection of court *objets d'art* carved in amber. One of its masterpieces is a standing-cup in the form of a nautilus shell, elaborately carved in low relief with miniature figures; it is signed by Jacob Heise and dated 1659. Not very different in quality is the wonderfully transparent tankard in the Waddesdon Bequest (Colour Pl. XVIA,B), the sides of which have nine emblematic figures representing the Vices and, in the centre of the domed lid, the royal arms of Sweden. A similar tankard but carved with the figures of the Virtues and a German inscription is among the Danish royal treasures in Rosenborg Castle, Copenhagen, while a third, belonging to the parish church of North Mimms in Hertfordshire, has the date 1659 carved on one of the panels. Even the base and the inside of the lid of the Waddesdon tankard have been skilfully carved, so that when the light shines through the amber, a strong three-dimensional effect is created by the reversed intaglio engraving – an effect so successfully achieved by the exponents of engraving on rock-crystals in Italy and in Prague. At what date this amber tankard left the Swedish royal household is not known but it was acquired from the Count Nostitz of Prague in the nineteenth century.

The portrait medal, so popular during the Renaissance, began in Italy in the fifteenth century with the famous Pisanello medal of the Byzantine Emperor, John VIII Palaeologus. During the sixteenth century outstanding artists, like Cellini and Leone Leoni in Italy and Dürer and Hans Reinhardt in Germany, contributed to its artistic and technical development; for example, the technique of casting medals for limited distribution was replaced during the sixteenth century by die-striking, so that, like coins, a far greater quantity could be produced for circulation. In the Bequest, there are a number of portrait medallions in wood and honestone which should be studied in relation to contemporary medallic art. The majority of these carvings are German, but one extraordinary piece, however, is quite outstanding, for it is carved in relief with an allegorical scene – not a portrait; because of its quality and style, it has been attributed to Peter Flötner (Fig.68). It depicts a king standing in the centre while from his right hand, in which he holds a sponge, a liquid drips to the ground; behind him are three courtiers, while in front a seated jester points to a distant hill where a man is about to be executed. The subject, together with a woodcut illustration, appeared in a book published in Paris in 1534 entitled *Emblematum flumen abundans*. This intriguing and sensitively carved relief reveals a strong Italian influence and dates from long after Flötner's Italian journey in 1520–2. Peter Flötner was one of those gifted artists of the Renaissance who so excelled in a number of fields – sculptor, stone-cutter, medallist, engraver, goldsmith, cabinet-maker, even architect. Born in Switzerland about 1485, Flötner worked mainly in Augsburg and Berne until after his return from Italy when he settled in Nuremberg, where he died in 1546. Although later versions in lead are known, the original, which was probably cast in a precious metal or bronze, is not recorded; indeed, this honestone relief may be an unfinished model, for it lacks the inscription beneath the scene.

One of the finest wood-carvings of the Renaissance preserved in the Bequest is too large to have been made as a model for a medal and may, therefore, not represent an intermediary stage in the production but be a final version – a portrait plaque in its

Fig. 68 Honestone relief carved with an allegorical scene comprising an execution (in the distance), a jester and a king squeezing a sponge in his right hand. By Peter Flötner, Nuremberg, *c*.1540. Diam. 2½in (6.4cm).

own right (Fig.69). It was carved in 1531 and depicts Wolfgang Thenn at the age of thirty-one seated on a wall in a very naturalistic pose and dressed in the height of fashion with an excess of slashings and ribbons. He lived in Salzburg, where his father was Master of the Mint to the Prince-Archbishop of Salzburg. The family's armorial bearings and crest are carved at the top of the panel, on either side of the inscription, and in the mountainous landscape in the distance a stag-hunt is in progress. The style of this landscape is typical of the Danube School of painting at this date but, despite the extremely high quality of this panel, it is difficult to attribute it to a particular artist of that region.

Perhaps the most important of all the small-scale carvings in wood in the Bequest are the two busts, traditionally attributed to Conrad Meit of Worms (Figs.70,71). They depict the artist's patron, Margaret of Austria, daughter of the Emperor Maximilian and Regent of the Netherlands, with her late husband, Philibert of Savoy, who had died in 1504. Conrad Meit, whose biographical details are far from well-established, is known to have worked from 1514 at the court of Margaret of Austria in Malines, and on 5 January 1518 there is an interesting record of a payment to Meit which reads: *'pour deux visages de bois à notre semblance, 8 philippas'*. In the Bayerisches Nationalmuseum in Munich there is a small wooden portrait head of Margaret of Austria, which comes from the famous Ambras collection of the Archdukes of Tyrol, and in the Berlin Museum there is an almost identical bust of Philibert of Savoy. However, the Berlin bust has suffered some damage, particularly to the brim of the hat, and so it lacks the

Fig.69 Pearwood portrait of Wolfgang Thenn, son of the Master of the Mint to the Prince-Archbishop of Salzburg, dated 1531. H. 6¾ in (17.1 cm).

curious hat-badge which can be seen on the Waddesdon Bequest bust and which depicts the figure of St Margaret and her dragon encircled by the inscription IE.NE.SCAI. As yet, the Burgundian source for this badge has not been traced, though its subject is a very obvious choice for the husband of Margaret of Austria (Fig.72).

Conrad Meit is often regarded as the greatest German wood-carver of the Renaissance, though only a handful of his works has survived to testify to his brilliance as a portraitist and sculptor. He was recorded in Antwerp in 1536 and died in 1550 or 1551, but these two busts are usually thought to date from the first ten years after he joined the court at Malines in 1514 and may possibly be related to a pair of marble busts (now lost) that Conrad Meit had begun for his royal patron, whose devotion to the memory of her late husband, Philibert, is well-attested. She went on to build as a memorial for herself and her young, lost husband, the most beautiful Gothic church of Brou with its

Figs. 70–1 (*Left and right*) Wood portrait busts of Philibert of Savoy (1480–1504) and Margaret of Austria (1480–1530) traditionally attributed to Conrad Meit, *c*.1515–25. Margaret, the daughter of the Emperor Maximilian, had married Philibert of Savoy in 1501, but his death in 1504 left her a grieving young widow devoted to his memory.

Fig. 72 (*Overleaf*) Detail of the hat jewel from the bust of Philibert of Savoy (Fig.70); St Margaret and the Dragon encircled by the inscription IE.NE.SCAI. The full significance has yet to be discovered.

stained glass and its encrusted canopied tomb, but her energy and diverse talents made her court the focal point of humanism in Northern Europe and the chief centre for men of letters and the arts until her death in 1530.

Unfortunately, the history of these two busts cannot be traced back with certainty beyond the early nineteenth century when, about 1817, they were bought in Vienna for 32 florins by the father of Sir Edgar Boehm, from whom they were purchased by Baron Anselm de Rothschild of Vienna. The shrewd connoisseurship of Baron Anselm and the subsequent generosity of his son, Baron Ferdinand, has saved these rare portraits, along with so many other important *objets d'art*, for posterity to study and enjoy. The present Waddesdon Room at the British Museum has been designed to show these magnificent treasures of the Renaissance courts of Europe in a manner that evokes something of the splendour of which they were originally a part.

Further Reading

This list, which relates to the order of chapters, is *not* a bibliography; it is a short selection of recent books that are readily available in London. Some contain extensive and useful bibliographies, which will serve as a guide for readers intending to study some aspect of the subject in greater detail.

Mrs James de Rothschild, *The Rothschilds at Waddesdon Manor* (London, 1979)

Hugh Trevor-Roper, *Princes and Artists: Patronage and Ideology at Four Habsburg Courts, 1517–1633* (London, 1976)

The Splendor of Dresden (Metropolitan Museum of Art, New York, 1978)

Hugh Tait, *The Golden Age of Venetian Glass* (British Museum, 1979)

Cipriano Piccolpasso's Three Books on the Potter's Art, eds. Ronald Lightbown and Alan Caiger-Smith (London, 1980)

Philippe Verdier, *Limoges Painted Enamels, The Frick Collection*, vol. VIII (New York, 1977)

Joan Evans, *A History of Jewellery, 1100–1870* (London, 2nd edn, 1970)

Priscilla E. Muller, *Jewels in Spain, 1500–1800* (New York, 1972)

Princely Magnificence: Court Jewels of the Renaissance, 1500–1630 (Debrett's Peerage Ltd, London, 1980)

J. F. Hayward, *Virtuoso Goldsmiths and the Triumph of Mannerism, 1540–1620* (London, 1979)

The Treatises of Benvenuto Cellini on Goldsmithing and Sculpture, trans. C. R. Ashbee (Dover Publications Inc., New York)

The Autobiography of Benvenuto Cellini, trans. and with introduction by George Bull (London)

John Shearman, *Mannerism: Style and Civilisation* (London, 1969)